SNAPSHOTS FROM MY CHILDHOOD

Karin Ann Tesdorf

2018 Karin Ann Tesdorf. All rights reserved.

Published by Tesdorf Design Sydney Australia.
This book is copyright. Apart from any fair dealing for the purpose of private study, research, criticism or reviews as, permitted under the Copyright Act, no part may be produced by any process without written permission.

ISBN : 978-0-9942320-3-8

This book is for my granddaughters, Ebba and Ellen Tesdorf.

I would like to thank my sister, Kerstin Hegarty, for all her valuable comments and advice. Not to mention reminding me of several incidents I had forgotten. Also, my husband Nicholas for his technical help and advice with the whole process.

Karin Ann, Cornwall 1964

INDEX

Chapter One : Assington Hall

Chapter Two : Wales

Chapter Three : London

Chapter Four : Post War Sweden

Chapter Five : Gränetorp, Summer 1948

Chapter Six : Landermere

Chapter Seven : More about Landermere

Chapter Eight : A Visit to France

Chapter Nine : A Bit More About Landermere

Chapter Ten : Stonelands

Chapter Eleven : Further Education in Stockholm

Chapter Twelve : Finland

Chapter Thirteen : Leningrad

Chapter Fourteen : Wine making.

Chapter Fifteen : Klares

Chapter Sixteen : Bertie

Chapter Seventeen : Granny

ASSINGTON HALL

Some of my earliest memories are from when my family lived in Assington Hall. The house was owned by Denis Dobson and John Platts-Mills, both of whom were barristers. John Platts-Mills was a New Zealander so the people they invited to leave London and the German Blitz Krieg of 1940 and come and share the country life, were either barristers or New Zealanders. Another family, John and Nell Hutton, came from New Zealand. My father, Bertie, was a barrister. My mother, Klares, was Swedish.

Each family had their own quarters but shared the dining room, sitting room and library. It was a type of communal living. There was a cook to do the cooking, Mrs Winyard and all the families had nannies to look after their children. The nannies didn't last long though. They were either called up to join the army or did so of their own accord, anticipating a more glamorous life in the WRENS or the WAAF.

Timothy and Joseph Platts-Mills were my closest playmates. Tim was the same age as me and Joey a year or so younger. Also, their quarters were directly beneath my family's. During the obligatory after lunch rest period, when we were confined to our bedrooms, Tim and Joey would often sneak upstairs to play with me. Invariably we heard footsteps on the stairs and the boys would rush and hide in a cupboard or under my bed. Their mother, Janet, would ignore my protests of ignorance and the boys were bustled back downstairs to carry on resting. On only one occasion had they not come up when Janet came bursting into my room.

"No, they aren't here," I replied truthfully, for once, to her question. I was sitting on the floor, playing quietly by myself.

She cast me a look of deep suspicion and looked under my bed and in the cupboard. I felt quite hurt that she had mistrusted me.

Roger Dobson was a year older than me and he had a sister who was three years younger, Zuleika. The Dobsons lived on the other side of the house so we never met up during our rest period.

The Second World War was in full swing and I remember that our mothers once spent the afternoon throwing bottles accross a paddock to practise throwing handgrenades at the enemy. The children tagged along and then ran and collected the bottles for the next round.

All our fathers were in the army and turned up every now and then in their khaki uniforms. Kerstin, from an early age, would rush up to any man in uniform crying "Daddy!" if we hadn't seen him for a while.

There was a small church attached to Assington Hall and Sheila Winyard, the cook's daughter who was several years older than me, would take me along to Sunday school. We were given booklets and every Sunday we were given a stamp to stick in it. One Sunday I was in bed with a cold and I begged Sheila to take my book with her and collect the stamp.

My favourite bedtime reading was *Babar the Elephant*. But I always skipped the page with the illustration of Babar sitting beside his dead mother, shot dead by cruel hunters.

Another of my favourite books was *Gone is Gone*. A philosophical look at life. In the book, a young farmer complained that his wife had a much easier time than him, staying at home, minding the baby and the cow and cooking the evening meal. The wife offered to swap places one day and of course, everything went wrong for the man. The dog ran off with the sausages, the cider ran out over the cellar floor and the baby tipped over the butter churn. When these mishaps occurred, the farmer shrugged his shoulders saying, " *gone is gone."*

In the evening the wife came home to find the cow dangling from the roof on the end of a rope. She cut the rope with her scythe and the cow landed on the ground. Her husband, attached to the other end, fell into the cooking pot. After that, he admitted that his wife's tasks were far more difficult than his.

Assington Hall was perfectly suited for Christmas. In the entrance hall was a large fireplace with enough room for Father Christmas to stand in and hand out presents. I was sorry for the older children who got clothes. I think that was when I was given my stuffed panda, who has been with me ever since. The atmosphere was memorable with the mysterious effects of candle light and the church choir singing Christmas carols. When it snowed we could go out and build snowmen and throw snowballs at each other.

Kerstin, my sister, was born during the time we lived at Assington. Bertie took me to visit Klares and the baby in hospital. My first impression of Kerstin was a mass of dark hair. Later her hair became a light brown, much lighter than mine.

At some point, Bertie appeared with an Alsation dog, Prince Polski. He would come bounding up to me and place his forepaws on my shoulders, sending me flying. He was quartered in the kennels in the yard but he was soon recruited and went off to do his bit in the army.

I am not sure how long we lived there. The next thing I knew, we were moving. Klares with Kerstin and me and Nell Hutton with her twin boys, Warwick and MacCailan, or Wocky and Cailey as they were called. Klares and Nell put as much distance as possible between us and the Second World War and moved to North Wales.

I believe all the fathers who were living at Assington Hall survived the war. John Platts-Mills set up a successful practice and became a Q. C. Some of the famous, or perhaps infamous, people he defended were the train robbers and the Kray brothers. Our families met occasionally after the war.

John Hutton became a well-respected artist. One of his best known projects was for the etched glass windows at Coventry Cathedral. The Cathedral, designed by Sir Basil Spence, stood alongside the ruins of the one that had been bombed during the war. John also designed and executed etched glass windows for New Zealand house in London, St Paul's Cathedral in Wellington, New Zealand and some of the Cunard liners. Our families shared houses at different periods after the war and Nell became one of Klares' oldest friends.

MONICA WILLIAMS, NELL HUTTON, THELMA DOBSON, K;ARES & JANET PLATTS-MILLS

KA, SHEILA WINYARD & ROGER DOBSON

KA & PANDA

KA & KLARES

WALES

Klares and Nell Hutton left Assington Hall in 1943 and moved to north Wales. They bought a small place, Utica Cottage, situated close to the village of Blaenau Ffestiniog and near the shores of lake Trawsfynydd. In the distance you could see Snowdon, the highest mountain in Wales and beside the cottage ran a one track railway line. A high embankment shielded us from the trains but you could hear them puffing past in the early hours of the morning. Preferable to sounds of air raid sirens and bombs falling and exploding. Not that we ever heard anything like that at Assington Hall.

A. S. Neil had evacuated his co-educational and controversial boarding school Summerhill, to Blaenau Ffestiniog. When I was four I was sent there. On my first morning a woman called Joan came striding into the dormitory, stark naked. She flung back the curtains to let in the morning light. This was an interesting start to boarding school life!

We went down to the dining room for breakfast where a rowdy mob had already gathered. Glancing up at the ceiling I noticed that it was dotted with pats of butter which had been thrown up and got stuck. I think food shortage was less severe in Wales, at least as far as butter was concerned.

I knew one of the other girls, Ann-Marie Sergeant. She had a Swedish mother like me and an English father. Also, a couple of my old play mates from Assington Hall, Tim and Joey Platts-Mills were there.

So there we all were at Summerhill, enjoying a warfree existence at Neil's famous school where children's views were listened to and to some extent they could decide what they did or didn't want to do, like go to lessons. Neil believed that the school should fit the child.

Everything at the school was run on democratic lines. Meetings were held once a week when complaints were voiced and rules were agreed on. Everyone had an equal vote. If some punishment was to be meted out for wrong doing, the children discussed what the punishment should be and voted for or against it. I imagine that this included bullying but I do remember being afraid of some of the older boys. One of them threw away my teddy bear when I was playing in the sand pit and it was never recovered. I was too afraid to bring this up at a meeting.

Not long after I started there, the younger children were moved to a separate house, away from the main school building and the older children. Our only contact then with the main school was when we were sent on errands to collect tins of porridge oats, our standard breakfast food.

School holidays were spent at Utica cottage with Klares and Kerstin, together with Nell, Cailey and Wocky. There was no electricity or running water indoors though there was an outdoor lavatory you could flush. This lavatory could be locked from the outside and it was my fervent ambition to catch Mrs Richards, the cleaning lady in there and lock the door. Somehow she was aware of my evil intentions and I never succeeded.

Water had to be collected in buckets from a well nearby. Every morning Klares used to go outside the back door and throw a bucket of cold water over herself. She did this for a while, till the milkman got to hear of it and timed his deliveries accordingly. Klares then had to content herself with ablutions in a metal tub in the kitchen.

Oil lamps and candles provided us with light. One evening the twins and I were working on a puzzle, heads bent over the table, engrossed in our task.

Suddenly Cailey let out a yelp and streaked off towards the kitchen, a living torch, flames leaping up from his hair. Nell appeared in the doorway and in a twinkling of an eye lifted up the front of her apron and smothered the flames. I was so impressed by her decisive action but strangely enough, I am the only one who remembers this event. Ever since then, it has been etched in my memory!

The train that ran past our house did not run on Sundays. During the summer we were able to walk along the track and pick wild strawberries that grew on the embankment. On our side of the embankment it was practically a sheer drop down to the ground level. Once Cailey decided to take his wheelbarrow up to the top but slipped and fell with loud screams and cries onto the concrete below.

"It's lucky he is screaming, you know he isn't dead," Klares observed. I am not sure that Nell appreciated this remark but then she could also make the odd unkind comment about Kerstin and me.

"Karin Ann goes to Cailey's head like strong wine!" She once complained to Klares.

Nowadays the little train from Blaenau Ffestiniog is run as a tourist attraction to Porthmadog. In those days it was standard public transport. We did not use it very often but once I was coming home from somewhere with Klares and my beloved panda. The luggage rack reminded me of a bunk bed so I put him up there to rest. I hopped off the train without a seconds thought and then let out a wail as the train puffed off down the track.

"Panda, panda's on the train!"

Klares quickly spoke to the ticket collector and in due course, panda was returned to me, none the worse for his adventure.

On another occasion, one of the male teachers from Summerhill, Tony Black, had a few drinks with the train driver and was allowed to drive the train home. As it was a one track line, there was no risk of meeting an oncoming train.

The surrounding countryside was very beautiful. The school sometimes took us for walks in the nearby forest. Gushing streams and waterfalls coursed down the rocks. It must have been autumn because the leaves were orange, brown and golden, on the trees and underfoot. Rain drops glistened on every surface, it was like a fairy tale world.

Round lake Trawsfynydd it was more open heath land with rocky outcrops and the odd sheep grazing. Klares and I had a long walk round the lake one day. I had found a jar of sugar coated children's sleeping pills in the medicine cabinet and consumed half a bottle. Afterwards I must have confessed to Klares what I had done. She rang the doctor who told her to give me a cup of weak tea and take me on a long walk and not to let me fall asleep.

My final memory from Wales is when I contracted ring worm at school and brought it home and passed it on to Kerstin. Luckily the twins were not infected as we would never have heard the end of it.

Klares took Kerstin and me up to London for some draconian treatment that was being used at the time, radiation, similar to the treatment of cancer. The treatment was available in a London clinic. Unfortunately, the same treatment was used for pimps and prostitutes to cure sexually transmitted diseases. The atmosphere at the clinic was grim and Dickensian. Lying on the couch,

KERSTIN, CAILEY, NELL, WOCKY, KA

A.S. NEIL

KERSTIN

TIMMY & JOEY PLATTS-MILLS & KA

with the enormous radiation machine over one's head, was not a pleasant experience.

We lost all our hair after that. Kerstin's hair grew back curly but I decided that I wanted to be a boy and kept my hair cut short. I called myself Newton, I have no idea why but after a couple of years I decided to become a girl again.

LONDON

Towards the end of the war, Nell and Klares had had enough of life in Wales and moved to London. There were still sporadic bombs being dropped but they rented a flat in Belsize Park, 43 Belsize Park Gardens. This was a residential area so less likely to attract the enemy's attention.

It was a large flat, consisting of the main entrance level and the floor above. There were two large bedrooms, two small bedrooms, a kitchen and dining room, bathroom and a playroom for the children upstairs. Two of us slept in the playroom. Our parents had the large bedrooms and we shared the kitchen and   dining room. Downstairs the families had separate sitting rooms and shared another large room where Nell and Klares had their weaving looms.

The basement level with the garden was occupied by an elderly couple. We soon gave the man the nickname of Mr Grumpy. I don't think that having four lively children living in the flat above was particularly peaceful. According to Nell, we were known as the Beasts of Belsize. The owners lived in the top floor flat.

In those days there were very few cars in London so we could play football and cricket in the street. We were close to Primrose Hill in one direction and Hampstead Heath in the other. Often we were taken there by an adult but sometimes we went by ourselves. Once Cailey and I took a tent to Primrose Hill and pitched camp there. I had taken Bertie's Lapp knife with me with its beautiful carved handle of reindeer horn and reindeer leather sheath. Sadly, I managed to lose it. A group of boys threatened us and we decamped in a hurry.

Another time, coming home from Hampstead Heath I was running down Haverstock Hill, not looking out for traffic. I nearly got hit by a car as I sped across one of the side streets. That taught me a lesson. Nowadays one is very careful to teach small children to look in both directions before crossing a road.

I think that four children got a bit much for the two mothers and so I was sent to boarding school again. This time Kingsmuir school near Sible Hedingham in Essex. The school was run by Lucy Francis, a close friend of Klares and a former associate of A. S. Neil, who also believed in progressive education. She based her school on Summerhill. We did not have to go to lessons if we didn't want to but I think most of us enjoyed learning. We had weekly meetings to decide on rules and punishments for minor crimes. I can't remember that we ever decided on rewards for good behavior or good team spirit or anything!

The twins and Kerstin went to The King Alfred school. A progressive day school in Golders Green. It was not quite so advanced as Summerhill or Kingsmuir school though. The children did have to go to lessons but rules were minimal and the children were encouraged to think independently. There was an underground train from Belsize Park to Golders Green and the twins and Kerstin quite happily took themselves off to school every day, no one thinking twice about it. That would not happen today!

By the end of 1945 when the second world war had finished, Klares decided it was time to go back to Sweden. She had not seen her sisters for over five years and London, with its rationing and bombed out houses was a very austere place to live. She took Kerstin with her and some friends took over our share of 43 Belsize Park Gardens. I was perfectly happy at boarding school and Bertie was stationed with the occupying forces in Germany. He had some involvement with the trials that took place in Nurenburg as he spoke German and French fluently and he was a barrister by profession.

A year later, when the family returned to London, I had to change schools. Bertie did not share Klares' conviction that Neil and Lucy had got it right as far as education was concerned. He wanted me to follow a more conventional school curriculum, finishing with a degree from a university. As it turned out, I did achieve this but by different means, an Art School degree rather than an academic one.

I started at St Mary's Town and Country school. The town school was just round the corner from us in Eton Avenue. Sarah White and one of her cousins were already going there, which was a good recommendation. Sarah was a cousin of Roger and Zuleika Dobson who had been at Assington Hall.

In January that year I had my first birthday party at home. Usually I was away at boarding school. I decided to have a fancy dress party.

One mother phoned me up, she sounded concerned. "My daughter's a bit plump, what do you think she should dress up as?"

KA READING

NORFOLK: CAILEY, KERSTIN, WOCKY & KA

SCHOOL MEETING
KA PRESIDING

I was just turning nine and I wracked my brains to be helpful. "What about Humpty Dumpty?"

The mother laughed and her daughter, Sally Bell, came dressed as a prince. She did not look especially fat. I doubt whether any child was fat in those days, thanks to food being in short supply. Klares went to great effort to provide successful food for the party, despite rationing still being in full force. Her *piece de resistance* were jelly clowns. These were elaborate concoctions of jelly and blancmange with bits and pieces for the eyes and nose, hats and ruffs. Each child got their own jelly clown, a real labour of love. We had eaten and were downstairs in the weaving room playing games. Klares was upstairs in the kitchen, dealing with the aftermath of the tea party when Timothy Platts-Mills stuck his head round the door.

"Anything left to eat?"

One of the children had been unable to come at the last minute so there was one jelly clown left over. Klares gave him the jelly clown and saw it vanish in a trice. She could not believe her eyes, after all the effort she had put into it. A few days later she contracted shingles and she always blamed Tim and his demolition of the jelly clown, without a seconds thought.

POST WAR SWEDEN

Christmas 1946 was the most boring Christmas I can remember. Klares and Kerstin were in Sweden and I was spending the holidays with my grandmother in Richmond. Her youngest sister, Hannah, took me to bazaars and a Christmas service at the local church but she was a bit strange. She was the youngest of eleven children which must have adversely affected her. Granny was the eldest so that probably explained her too. My father's youngest brother, Harold, was around but he was more interested in his wife-to-be so I didn't see much of him.

Granny had to wake me up on Christmas morning. Usually I was awake early, rootling among the presents in my pillowcase at the end of the bed. Klares had sent a parcel with lots of nice things from Sweden. I remember a marzipan pig and a wooden Christmas tree that fitted together like a cross, among other presents.

My parents were not very fond of Granny. Both Kerstin and I have come to realise over the years that she always tried to do her best. That Christmas she had managed to buy a meccano set for me. I had once wanted to become a boy but I was not interested in construction toys. Hopefully I was able to seem pleased with the present!

I returned to Kingsmuir School for the Spring Term and just before Easter I came back to London. Granny took me on the train to Harwich to catch the boat to Gothenburg in the south of Sweden. I was so excited. I was going to travel by myself as an unaccompanied minor and I was going to see my family again.

Besides which, I was going to experience Sweden, a country Klares had often talked about and her life growing up in Stockholm. Sweden had not been involved in the Second World War so everything would be quite different there.

The beautiful white ship gleamed in the sun. The Suecia, one of the Swedish Lloyd Lines, the start of my adventure. Granny put me in the charge of a stewardess, a middle-aged slightly frazzled looking woman who I hardly saw during the trip and waved me off. The voyage lasted two nights so I had a whole day to explore. I must have been in first class as I had a free run of the ship and could go wherever I wanted to.

Nowadays it seems strange that a young child would be sent off on a ship by themselves but I suppose things were different then. After all, parents in London had sent their young children to the country to stay with complete strangers. Anything to avoid the bombing but they had no idea where the children were going to end up or who would be looking after them.

Life on board was full of interesting and exciting things to do. I made friends with one of the engineers down in the engine room. He showed me all the enormous, pulsating machinery and roaring flames that drove the ship along. I don't remember coming across any other children on board and the only people I spoke to were those who sat at the same table at meal times. They were impressed when I managed to eat four eggs for breakfast on the last morning. Coming from war-torn Britain, I just couldn't believe my eyes at the abundance of food, attractively laid out for everyone to help themselves.

Bertie was there on the quay to meet me, looking very handsome in his khaki uniform and black beret. I rushed down the gangplank to throw myself into his arms.

"I ate four eggs for breakfast!"

From Gothenburg we boarded the train for Stockholm. Bertie bought me a bag of sweets for the journey, six or seven hours. The carriage was full. The other passengers were all very friendly, no doubt interested to see a British soldier with his young daughter in their midst.

I handed round the bag of sweets and that triggered off a huge response. Possibly aware that England was suffering severe food shortages, I was soon inundated with fruit and sweets and goodness knows what. I was amazed by the bounty. Things were certainly quite different in Sweden than war-torn, heavily rationed England!

It was dark when we reached Stockholm and my first impression of that beautiful city was a giant illuminated advertisement for Pommac on the side of a building, complete with realistic bubbles. Pommac is a carbonated apple drink, still available today. We got a taxi to my aunt's house in Djursholm, a northern suburb of Stockholm. I was given a large stick of peppermint rock, red and white, like the Brighton variety. In Swedish it is called 'Polka Gris.'

We spent several happy months in Sweden, living with my aunt Viveka and cousin Nils. Bertie visited from time to time. It was a bit closer for him to travel to Stockholm from Germany and we spent a long weekend together in a hotel in Södertälje, by a lake.

Kerstin had already learnt to speak Swedish and for a while she acted as my interpreter. But I soon picked it up too, the way children do. Klares had always sung songs to us in Swedish, despite being tone deaf, so it was not a completely foreign language.

We had beautiful weather in August that year. The sun shone and we swam in the lake which was separated by a field from aunt Viveka's house on Tyrvägen, Ekebysjön.

We played with the neighbour's children, especially the Norbecks. They had four girls and a son, Johan, who was a few years older than me. Kerstin and I always felt welcome at their house, even though the girls were somewhat older than us. Monika (Mokka) who was the youngest, was probably 16 or 17 years old. They all had boyfriends and in the long drawn out summer evenings we often played hide and seek or kick the tin in their large, overgrown garden.

One afternoon we were invited to the prenuptial party for Annika, the oldest daughter. We had had very little to do with her, she had probably been too busy with all the arrangements for her wedding. Klares bought six eggcups as a present and entrusted the gift wrapped present to me. As we were leaving the house, Nils, carrying the parcel entrusted to him by Viveka and I started arguing about something. We chased each other, using the parcels as implements to whack the other about with. The adults stepped in and order was restored but when Annika opened our present, four of the eggcups were broken. The contents of the Granlund's parcel were uninjured. Klares was not amused! I had to apologise of course and the broken eggcups were replaced and I carried the slightly smaller parcel to the Norbeck's house without further damage.

We were not invited to the wedding but we lined up along the road leading to Danderyd's church and saw the bride and her father being transported in an open carriage, drawn by two white horses, all decked out with wild flowers. The bride wore a silver crown on her head and looked like a fairy princess. I think this was the first wedding Kerstin and I had seen and it created an everlasting impression.

In September we made the return journey, this time on a Russian boat. We left from Stockholm with a whole posse of relations to wave us off. One of them gave us a large box of chocolates for the journey.

The ship was big and we were not allowed down in the engine room. The crew didn't speak much English. The steward who waited on us at table was called Dmitri and wore a scruffy white jacket and brown carpet slippers. We learnt to say *'spaceba'*, thank you, *'mollakol'*, milk and '*chai*', tea. The food was Russian and probably basic, not like the meals on board The Suecia. The voyage took several days, across the Baltic Sea and through the Kiel Canal in Germany.

Entering the canal, everyone was on deck, curious to see what the country, our recent enemy, looked like. It looked bleak. Signs of bombing everywhere, black cranes stretching up alongside the docks. Down below on the quay, we saw three children, a boy and two little girls, legs like matchsticks.

Kerstin and I decided to give them our enormous box of Swedish chocolates. We rushed down to our cabin to collect it, hoping the children would still be there when we got back. They were, gazing up at the luxurious looking ship, a stark contrast to their post war existence.

"Here!" We threw the box and it landed beside them.

They immediately bent down to investigate the contents and the boy looked up and waved to us. We waved back, I think we were crying. We had been lucky not to be on the losing side.

SÖDERTÄLJE: KA, KLARES, KERSTIN & NILS

GRÄNETORP, SUMMER 1948

Gränetorp was the name of the timber cottage my cousin Nils' grandmother, Tante Tecla, had had built for her family in 1912. It was in a forest at the edge of a lake, not far from the small town of Gränna. Gränna lies beside a much larger lake called Vättern and is famous for the red and white striped mint sweet, Swedish polka gris. Tante Tecla looked pretty ancient in those days. Nils has a photograph of her when she was well over ninety, going for a ride on the back of his motorcycle. A true Viking.

The main access to Gränetorp was by boat. Gränetorp had its own jetty and a motorboat. Besides this, it looked the epitome of a small Swedish cottage, straight out of a fairy tale with grass growing on the roof and hearts cut out of the wooden shutters.

In the summer of 1948 Klares rented a small one roomed shack near by. It had a veranda in front and basic cooking and ablution arrangements. The veranda was furnished with a table and chairs so that was our dining room. Bertie was still in the army with the occupational forces in Germany and he only came for the odd weekend.

Every morning we were woken up by Nils' small dachshund Tommy, who came racing over from Gränetorp to bark at the hedgehogs who lived under our shack. We adored Tommy and were always glad to see him but Nils was never far behind to take him home again. He obviously felt that Tommy was being disloyal.

That summer the sun shone every day. The forest was full of blueberries. We picked and ate them and smeared the juice all over our bodies so we had to jump into the lake to wash ourselves. I swam, a basic dog paddle but Kerstin had not yet learnt to swim. Nils could swim of course. His home in Stockholm was near a lake and children had swimming lessons there from an early age.

In those days you celebrated names days rather than birthdays. Karin day was in the beginning of August and Klares invited Tante Tecla over with her daughter Tyra, Viveka and Nils for afternoon tea.

GRÄNETORP

KA & TOMMY

She dressed us up as wood nymphs and trolls and we had cake and coffee or juice. I probably received a few small presents too. Names days have the added advantage that you may have several and no one talks about your age.

Klares enrolled Kerstin and me in swimming classes at an hotel, situated a little further round the lake. We sat on a sandy beach and practised swimming movements with our arms. I can't remember that we ever practised in the water. Here I became friendly with an older girl, Anna, who invited me to the hotel for tea one day. I didn't invite her back to our place, maybe I felt our living quarters were a bit too primitive.

Mostly we played with Nils and a few children who were staying with a farmer on the other side of the forest. We had a couple of flat-bottomed boats you could paddle around in and we paddled over to a small island not too far from the shore. Here we fished and cooked the fish over a fire. Nils was able to light fires. He was a sea scout so he had learnt to light fires along with tying knots and all the other useful things they teach you in scouts.

One day Viveka and Klares decided to do a cycling trip round an island, Visingsö, which lay in lake Vättern. There was a ferry from Gränna that took you there. Kerstin was too young to cycle that distance so she rode behind Klares on the back carrier. The island was quite large, we cycled through a couple of villages and had a look at some churches. In one of them, Kerstin spotted some attractive brass numbers, highly polished, laid out ready to be put up on a board to let people know which hymns were to be sung. In a twinkling of an eye she had picked one up and stuffed it in her knickers.

We carried on with our cycling tour, stopping off for a picnic and a swim in the middle of the day. We were having a look at another old church when suddenly we heard a loud clanging noise. Unfortunately the brass number had fallen out of Kerstin's knickers on to the stone floor. Nils and I thought it was funny. Viveka was less amused.

"We will have to go back and return it," she looked serious.

Well, of course we had to do that and we did. The church was closed when we got there but we left the number by the front door, a safe a spot as any in those days.

Another day Anna, my friend from the hotel, asked Kerstin and me to come out rowing with her in the afternoon. She was probably about twelve years old and able to manage a rowing boat. In

VIVEKA, KA & KERSTIN

DRESSED AS TROLLS

those days one didn't bother with life jackets for children and we seemed to have very little adult supervision. Klares was probably quite happy that Anna was with us.

We rowed to the island and then carried on, gliding into the water lily patch near the shore. Both Kerstin and I stretched out to pick the flowers. The next minute there was a splash and Kerstin disappeared over the side of the boat, only her long hair floating on the surface. With great presence of mind, Anna grabbed her hair and was able to pull her back into the boat.

Poor Kerstin! It was a nasty shock for her and a nasty shock for me too. Anna rowed the boat back to the hotel and then we all hurried back to our shack to find Klares and tell her what had happened.

"Lucky she has long hair! I just saw her hair floating on the water and I pulled her out!" Anna explained.

I don't remember Klares' reaction, she was probably horrified but at least we were there, safe and sound. I think Kerstin learnt to swim quite soon after that little incident.

LANDERMERE
(The setting for one of the Swallows and Amazons books.)

When we moved to Landermere, a tiny hamlet on an estuary on the Essex coast, I was delighted. We had lived in London for a few years and even though I went to boarding school and life in Belsize Park Gardens was not too restrictive, I longed to live in the country.

Kerstin and I stayed with Granny in Richmond, while the move took place. Then Bertie collected us one afternoon and we caught a train heading north-east, to Thorpe-le-Soken. In those days trains belched steam and soot and the carriages were timber lined with brass fittings and wool upholstery. Nowadays the line is electrified, the carriages are just as dirty and everything is plastic and vinyl.

My corgi dog Foxy was with us of course and we could hardly wait for the first glimpse of our new home.

We had to change at Colchester for the branch line to Clacton, getting off the train at Thorpe-le-Soken, the nearest village to Landermere. The last part of the trip, two and a half miles, was by taxi and the last half mile was along a private road or cart track.

The King's Head, our new home, was once a pub. It was a black, two-story weatherboard building, nestled beside a narrow strip of sandy beach. The grey-blue water of the estuary sparkled in the setting sun. It was obviously high tide, at low tide the water was just a trickle in a sea of mud.

A mad scramble as we tumbled out of the car, dog barking frenziedly. Being a cattle dog, he liked the herd to stay together.

Klares appeared at the front door, smiling in welcome. "Come up and see your bedroom."

Kerstin and I shared a room, exposed timber beams painted white, pink walls and plenty of space for all the furniture that had been sent down from London.

"The Huttons have invited us for dinner."

Klares was helping Bertie carry up the suitcases. The Huttons had arrived in Landermere a few days before us and had moved in to a cottage opposite the King's Head.

"Hello! When did you get here?" Cailey appeared, coming up the staircase. "Come and see our house. We've got separate bedrooms. Karin Stephen is going to take us out sailing tomorrow!"

It was still the school holidays, early September perhaps and on our second weekend in this new territory, the twins and John Morris, a friend from Belsize Park and I decided to take the rubber dinghy and explore. Foxy came too, which was why I had a packet of dog biscuits with me.

The tide was out, channels of water separated numerous small islands dotted round the estuary. Far away in the distance was the North Sea. Dykes separated the estuary from the surrounding fields, some of them occupied by cows. Every now and then, Foxy's natural instincts got the better of him and he tried to round them up. But then he remembered that we were his first responsibility and he would return to make sure no one was straggling behind.

"Come on, we can carry the dinghy to the Hard and then paddle over to some of those large islands." Cailey and John carried the dinghy between them.

"We might find another heron." Wocky had found a poor bedraggled heron a few days earlier and brought it home to recover. He called it Hereward but unfortunately it did not survive in captivity.

We walked along the top of the dyke and then crossed over to a well-worn track leading to the Hard, an area where it was possible to launch the dinghy and explore some of the larger islands.

It was only a two-man dinghy so Cailey and John took it in turns to ferry the party across from island to island. Progress was slow but we managed to make our way, island hopping, before we realised that the tide had steadily been coming in and there was a strong current against us. The distance between the islands had become quite considerable.

"We won't be able to paddle back to where we came from!" John and Cailey both agreed that it would be too risky.

"We'll have to wait till the tide goes out again," I was stating the obvious.

THE KING'S HEAD

BERTIE & KARIN STEVENS

FOXY

"That'll take hours! Klares and Nell will get worried!" Wocky looked worried himself.

"Maybe they'll send out a search party?" John was optimistic.

We discussed our situation but there was nothing much to be done. I handed round the dog biscuits, they didn't taste too bad. We tried to light a fire, thinking we could attract someone's attention with the smoke but the matches had got wet. We kept an eye on the water level but the tide was still coming in. There was not much to explore on the island either, more or less a grassy knoll with a couple of trees on it, rising up above the high tide mark. This was probably the only time we ever set foot on it.

I don't remember how long we were marooned but suddenly we spotted a man striding along the dyke in the far distance.

"Help, we're stuck, we can't get away!" We all waved frantically and Foxy barked.

He waved back in response. We couldn't hear what he said but he turned back in the direction he had come.

"That was Nigel Henderson. He's probably gone to get a boat."

The twins had met Nigel recently, he was married to Judith, one of Karin Steven's daughters.

Sure enough, Nigel had been roped in to look for us and in a little while he reappeared, this time in a rowing boat. We were soon back at the Landermere beach, with much laughing and joking on his side.

I always thought that our mothers had taken the whole affair quite calmly. Luckily Nigel had been around, he and Judith only came for visits on odd weekends. Later, Kerstin told me that Klares had been terribly upset and probably Nell too, so Nigel Henderson was a complete God-send.

MORE ABOUT LANDERMERE

My family moved to Landermere in 1949. Landermere was a collection of houses on an estuary on the Essex coast, not far from Frinton, Clacton-on-sea and Walton. A rutted cart track led to the hamlet. There were five cottages on one side of the track, known as the coastguard cottages, one of which was called 'Gull Cottage'. Facing them was a larger house which had a timber annexe in front, 'The King's Head'. Further down the track was a big garden, surrounded by a hedge with a house and bungalow standing on the property. Colonel Balfour and his sister Mrs. Milne lived here; he lived in the house, she in the bungalow.

The estuary, bordering one side of the garden of the King's Head, filled with water at high tide. When the tide was out there were mud flats with small islands here and there. Below the King's Head was a small beach with some timber posts sticking up out of the mud, the remains of a quay. Klares used to execute beautiful swallow dives from the top of the tallest post.

According to my research on Google, the quay was owned by the lord of the manor, Richard Rigby in 1781. It was he who built the inn, The King's Head and the row of cottages. The inn was subsequently purchased by a George Munnings who commanded the revenue cutter 'Repulse', much feared by the local smugglers who operated from their fishing smacks.

Legend has it, that the crew of the old sailing barges had worked out a routine whereby the barge captains could dodge the customs men at Landermere by pausing at nearby Skippers Island to shelter there with their contraband. They returned to their vessels docked at the quay under the cover of darkness.

The King's Head lost its licence in 1913 because of its reputation as a notorious smugglers' haunt or maybe because someone was killed there. Since then the approach to the quay has silted up and barges can no longer navigate in those waters. Landermere lapsed into a Sleeping Beauty hibernation and it is just as isolated and unspoiled to this day.

Karin Stephen, sister-in-law to Virginia Woolfe, was the owner of the King's Head and the coast-guard cottages at the time we moved there. She was our landlady and would appear from time to time, staying in the main part of the King's Head. We lived in the timber annexe, a two-story building with two bedrooms upstairs and a sitting room and large kitchen with bathroom and scullery attached, downstairs. The Hutton family lived in Gull cottage.

Three of the other cottages were rented out to people on holiday there, usually friends of ours; a local family, the Bearders, occupied the remaining cottage. They had no children and our paths only crossed when Foxy got in a fight with their dachshund. The twin's spaniel usually joined in and I have memories of Foxy pulling from one end and Howie from the other. Buckets of water separated them, followed by profuse apologies.

Outdoor activities at Landermere centered round the water. We swam, we learned to sail we rowed. Kerstin and I and Sarah White, another family friend, saved up and for ten pounds we bought a heavy timber rowing boat. We christened her Boadicea, in reference to the local queen of the Celtic Iceni tribe, who had fought against the Romans. She was useful for island hopping when the tide was high.

Karin Stephen was a keen sailor and was anxious to get Bertie and the twins to come sailing with her. She didn't have much faith in the competence of girls but we were useful for hanging on to the jib or bailing out. Once I was out sailing with Klares and Nell and some of the other children. Foxy was desperate to come with us but my mother was not having a dog in the boat. He ran up and down on the shore, barking frantically. Suddenly he leapt into the waves and started dog paddling after us, the first time he ever swam.

"Stop! We must pick him up! He'll drown!" I screamed.

There was nothing else for it but to heave to and let me fish the valiant little creature out of the sea. He was absolutely delighted at having caught up with us and loved swimming ever after. He had the most elegant dive, front legs stretched out, a smile from ear to ear as he joined us in the water.

Summers were the best time of year at Landermere. We were free all day and various friends from London would be staying in one of the cottages. Dodo and Eric White with their daughter Sarah, the Morris family with John, Carol and Stevie, Basil and Joan Spence with Gillian and John and the McGibbons with Hamish, Janet and Robert.

Our parents had cars, practically vintage, pre-war numbers, but we usually did things without our parents and rode our bicycles. There was very little traffic on the roads in the early fifties and it was quite safe for children to be out cycling round the country-side.

One summer we played a lot of tennis at a local court in Walton. We must have taken it quite seriously as we organised a tennis competition, roping in any adult who knew how to play. The Spence family were Scottish and very competitive. They would only partner each other and won the tournament with ease.

Another summer some girl guides came and camped in a nearby field. Kerstin dressed up in my old Girl Guide uniform and bravely set off to deliver a note to them. She met a couple who saluted her in correct girl guide fashion but not having actually been a guide herself, she didn't know she was supposed to salute back. She quickly gave them the note and ran. We had asked them to meet us at the Red Barn at midnight. Later, a couple of guides came and delivered a note with an alternative suggestion and it ended up with us joining them in the middle of the night and sitting round their campfire, singing songs and drinking cocoa.

We had pitched a tent in our garden so we wouldn't have to tell our parents what we were up to. When we finally got home and crawled into our tent, we noticed that one of the Bearders was watching out of an upstairs window. I expect we told our families next morning but I don't think they were too worried.

We organised concerts, produced a local newsletter called The Landermere Times and now and then held dances in our sitting room. Much to the detriment of the carpet! Dodo White taught us how to do The Charleston and next morning there were little piles of wool all over the floor and not much left in the carpet. We had to roll it up for all subsequent dancing occasions. The boys were too embarrassed to ask us to dance with them so we drew up lists and everyone got a turn at dancing with everyone else.

Klares and Nell found a recipe for making beer. I remember Bertie saying to a guest once, "Try some Landermere mud!" laughing his head off.

I probably tried some and that might be the reason I was never very keen on beer. Their wine was more successful and quite potent. It had one of the guests stretched out on the garden path, giggling as she gazed up at the stars.

"I just had to lie down!" she explained.

GULL COTTAGES

KERSTIN & THE TWINS

LANDERMERE

A VISIT TO FRANCE

The year was 1949, or thereabouts. I was at boarding school, St Mary's Town and Country School, near Rugby, in Warwickshire. The school was housed in a large country house called Stanford Hall which was leased, together with the surrounding land from an elderly couple. They were Catholics and they lived in the Dower House on the boundaries of the estate.

The school children were a mixture of Catholic, Church of England, Agnostic and maybe even Jewish religions. The Catholics were the most noticeable as they had to go off to church before breakfast on certain saints days. They also got invited to afternoon tea at the Dower House from time to time. I went along once, I'm not quite sure why. I think maybe someone was sick and I was allowed to fill in.

A high proportion of the children came from families whose parents were divorced or whose fathers had been killed in the war. Among my friends, I was the only one who still had both their parents alive and living together.

The headmistress, Mrs. Paul, was French. Her husband was German. She was the driving force behind the enterprise and used to divide her time between London, The Town School and us in the country. It was always more pleasant when she was away. One term I was sleeping in a dormitory above her sitting room. A huge crystal chandelier hung from the ceiling and if any child got out of bed, the crystals would shiver and Mrs Paul would be up in a flash to order us to stand in line outside her sitting room door for half an hour or so.

Mr Paul taught us German and in appearance, was definitely the underdog compared with his wife. He drove a ramshackle old car, which one of the boys unkindly said was held together with wire and string.

One of my classmates, who also slept in the same dormitory, was a French girl, Evonne Mason-Forrestiere. She came over from Paris every term. Her father had been killed in the war. Four of us shared the same dormitory and had done so ever since we started at the school, a couple of terms previously. Friendships waxed and waned. Sometimes one was best friends with one girl, sometimes another.

For a while, Evonne and I were good friends and I suggested that she come and stay with my family for part of the holiday and then I would travel with her to Paris. Letters were written, our-parents agreed and we started off the summer holidays at Landermere.

Hopscotch was a popular pastime that year. We swam of course when the tide was in but when the tide was out, there was enough sandy beach for endless games of hopscotch. The members of our gang that summer were Cailey and Wocky, Sarah White and John Morrison besides Kerstin and myself.

Sometimes we were driven to Frinton, a very genteel seaside resort where one was not allowed to picnic on the greensward and where there was a row of little timber changing huts to rent, overlooking the beach. Occasionally my parents or one of their friends would hire one for the day and it felt very luxurious. Apart from being able to change in comfort you could sit on the front step and sunbathe, eat ice creams and even the odd sandwich. You could also swim; there was always water at Frinton.

Evonne stayed with us for two or three weeks and then we set off for Paris. She was a year older than me and had done the trip a number of times so we travelled on our own. Bertie took us to Waterloo station to catch the boat train without any qualms.

We were fine of course. Evonne's mother met us at Gare du Nord and took us home to her apartment in a respectable arrondisement. It was very elegant, on two or three levels with a mezzanine level, the library, running round the sitting room. Evonne had an older brother and he helped entertain us, taking us to the tomb of the Unknown Soldier and the Eiffel Tower. The light on top of the Eiffel Tower revolved and shone into my bedroom at night.

One morning we went to buy something in a local grocery shop. A large American woman was there.

"Have you got Heinz baked beans?"

The shopkeeper stared at her. She repeated the question, louder and then a third time, getting louder and angrier by the minute. She obviously didn't even know any basic phrases in French.

Perhaps Evonne intervened at this stage and did a bit of interpreting.

After a few days in Paris, Evonne's mother had arranged for us to stay with some friends of hers who lived at Senlis, just outside Paris. The family had a few children and we went to the local swimming pool together, we also went riding. Evonne's mother came to stay for the weekend and took us riding in the forest, immaculately attired, riding sidesaddle. She was a very good horsewoman.

The French meals intrigued me. Fish, meat, vegetables all served as separate courses and wine for the children, diluted with water. I can remember feeling shocked. Thank goodness my outlook has broadened!

We were invited to tea one afternoon to one of their neighbours, a branch of the pretenders to the French throne, the Bourbons I think. Nothing has come of their aspirations over the intervening years, as far as I know.

For some reason my return date had not been fixed when I left home and I wrote to my parents and told them I would be arriving on Thursday, 27th August. The day, Thursday, was correct but not the date, 27th August was a Wednesday. This time I would be travelling by myself but I was not worried. Evonne's brother made me some sandwiches for the journey and asked if I had a boyfriend.

"Foxy!" I replied, embarrassed by the question.

"That's her dog!" Evonne was scornful but in actual fact neither of us had a boyfriend, even though we went to a co-educational school.

I arrived back at Waterloo station safely and there was Bertie, waiting to meet me, smiling.

"We didn't know whether you were coming yesterday or today."

I had realised my mistake, but too late to let them know and I was very contrite.

Many, many years later Kerstin told me that Klares had been quite hysterical when I hadn't turned up on Wednesday, imagining the worst. I don't know why they hadn't rung up. Probably they didn't have the Mason-Forrestier's phone number. No mobile phones either; life was far more unpredictable and exciting!

STANFORD HALL

EIFFEL TOWER

RIDING AT SENLIS

A BIT MORE ABOUT LANDERMERE

Just reading over the two chapters on Landermere, I realise there is quite a bit I have missed out about growing up there.

After a couple of years living at the King's Head, my parents persuaded Karin Steven to let us rent one of the coastguard cottages. It had previously been rented to Eduardo Paolozzi who, despite his name was Scottish and who became a well known sculptor. For some reason he gave up his lease on the cottage and at long last Kerstin and I could have separate bedrooms. Her bedroom was above the kitchen and she could either go through my bedroom or via a trapdoor by a stepladder, permanently in position in the kitchen.

The annexe had had its drawbacks. It was a bit too close to our landlady. Karin Steven had taken a liking to Bertie and would come prowling round to the kitchen, looking like one of the Troll mothers in a John Bauer fairy tale. She wore a woollen cap on her head with her wiry grey hair spilling out round her face. Some kind of loose jumper or jacket over a shapeless skirt with gum boots on her feet. Bertie would try and hide but he was not always successful.

Our 'fridge' a small cupboard with perforated metal sides and door, hung outside on a wall, just below her bedroom window. Karin was in the habit of emptying her chamber pot out of the window, missing the fridge only by inches. Another unusual feature was that Bertie had cut a slot in the back door for the mail. The lavatory was right beside the door and you were quite likely to get a lap full of letters without any warning. I don't know if the postman knew where the mail was landing.

We had a lovely time moving all our stuff, helped by Sarah. The adults moved the big pieces of furniture but we had enough goods and chattels to ferry across the road to keep us occupied for a whole day. We were living in the cottage the day King George VI died, in February 1952. I was at home from school with tonsillitis when our local doctor paid a house call. He rushed into the sitting room where I was all rugged up with blankets on the sofa and pounced on the radio.

"The King is dead," he announced as he turned on the radio and fiddled with the dials.

People were shocked. George VI was only 54 years old. He had been a good King and, together with his wife and daughters, had supported his subjects during the darkest moments of World War 2. At the time, I was not fully aware of the seriousness of what the country had gone through but I was still upset by his death. I remember a very poignant photo in one of the newspapers of his mother, the dowager Queen Mary, his wife Elizabeth and daughter Elizabeth, the future Queen, all dressed in black with black veils. They looked incredibly sad.

Sarah's father Eric took a great interest in our acting aspirations. He was somewhat of a writer, alongside his job at the Arts Council and became a well known authority on Stravinsky. He later published a book on the Russian composer. As children we were not aware of his public profile but we loved the clerihews he wrote in our autograph books.

In mine he wrote: *Though her aunt can't cancan*
Karin Ann can.
And for Kerstin: *It's past doubt*
That Kerstin will be first in
And last out.

Eric wrote a play for us to perform, something about space craft and landing on the moon with parts specially written for all the children but I don't remember when we performed it.

Through his position on the Arts Council, Eric was able to book the Chairman's box at Covent Gardens for opera and ballet performances. He once took us and Sarah and the twins to a performance of *Let's Make an Opera* by Benjamin Britten. The epitome of my opera experiences however, was when he and Dodo took me to see Verdi's *La Traviata*. I sat in the box and wished the opera would never finish.

One summer, Geoffrey Cox, a New Zealander like the Huttons, stayed with his family in Frinton. Geoffrey was a famous journalist and had been a war correspondent during the Spanish Civil War and World War 2. After the war he was editor for the News Chronicle and later he became editor and chief executive of ITN television. He and his wife Cecily had two boys, Peter and Patrick and twin girls, Rosamund and Evelyn. Geoffrey had decided to shoot a film, based on Landermere and its smuggling history, using the local talent to act the parts.

Kerstin was later given a copy of the film but I have only a vague memory of the plot. I believe that the twins and John Morris were cast as smugglers. Kerstin and I were barmaids at the King's Head and Sarah was the heroine who overheard our discussions with the smugglers and raced across the dykes in a large hat to alert the excise men, Peter and Patrick Cox. The twin girls were probably too young to take part. Landermere provided a good back drop with its built up dykes and estuary and the notorious King's Head, suitably painted black.

That was a particularly fine summer, the sun shone every day and the Coxes generously allowed us to share their beach hut at Frinton.

Nell and Klares had a cleaning lady, Mrs Mayhew, to enable them to devote more time to their weaving. Heals in London was still buying their Scandinavian rag rugs and they also had some private commissions. Even then, sugar, coffee, tea and a few other things were still rationed and by encouraging Kerstin and me not to take sugar with our tea or on our cereal, Klares was able to swap some of her sugar rations for coffee and tea rations with Mrs Mayhew. That was a good thing, as far as I am concerned, with lasting benefits!

Mrs Mayhew had a son Joe, who must have been 20 or thereabouts. Joe had obviously recently got his drivers licence and had bought himself an old car, which he took to driving at reckless speed up and down our local Landermere road, scattering gravel and mud in all directions.

"He's looking for a girl friend," Mrs Mayhew confided in Klares.

"He's trying to attract you," Klares mischievously passed on this piece of gossip to me.

I was outraged. "I'm not interested in him, we've never even spoken to each other!"

Thinking back on it, Joe was probably just practising his driving skills on our relatively deserted stretch of road. I am sure there were plenty of girls of his own age living locally who he had his eye on. I was only 13 after all. Meanwhile I developed a crush on one of the boys who attended Colchester Grammar School for boys.

I went to Colchester High School for girls at this stage and I saw him waiting to catch a train at the station every afternoon, standing with a group of boys. I travelled with a group of girls and we discussed how I could get to know him. Dropping my hanky as I walked past seemed a good ploy. He would of course pick it up and we could start talking. I discovered his name and asked the twins about him as they also went to the Grammar School. Sadly the report was not good. According to the twins he was not popular, for various reasons.

I stopped thinking about him but then one day, at the station, he came running after me with my hanky which I had dropped, though not on purpose. I had completely lost interest in him by now, in fact I scarcely remembered who he was. I just took the hanky and thanked him and ran off to catch my train.

At some point, Klares decided to send Kerstin over to Sweden to stay with our aunt Viveka for a few months. She thought it would be beneficial to separate us as I was inclined to tease Kerstin. I was the bad older sister. The family took her to Harwich and like me, she was entrusted into the care of a stewardess. Jan Wallinder, Klares' cousin, met her at Gothenberg and put her on the train to Stockholm.

Viveka somehow discovered that Kerstin had not been christened and arranged to have this carried out in Sweden, presumably with our parents' blessing. This was a big worry for me when she returned to England and told me of her new status. I knew Klares had been christened, I assumed that Bertie hadn't but I didn't want to be shuffled off into outer darkness while Kerstin and Klares were in Paradise.

I decided that I wanted to be christened too and Sarah thought she might as well join me. We were christened in the local church at Thorpe-le-Soken and Sarah's mother Dodo, kindly agreed to be my godmother. Bertie did not come to the church for the ceremony but years later, when Alex was christened at the church at Danderyd in Sweden, Bertie was there.

During our last year of living full time at Landermere, Kerstin passed her 11plus exam and joined me at Colchester County High School. We wore navy blue uniforms, gym slips, blazers and velour hats and every day we cycled into Thorpe-le-Soken to catch the train to Colchester. I don't remember there being any buses and more often than not we used our bicycles to get anywhere, especially all the local villages like Thorpe, Frinton, Clacton and Walton.

One day I was home on my own, probably a weekend and Mr Bearder came and stuck his head round the door.

"Your sister's had an accident and come off her bike," he informed me.

"Is she okay?" I gasped.

"Well, she can talk," he admitted, somewhat reluctantly I thought.

Shortly after a neighbour arrived with Kerstin, mud spattered and bedraggled and in a state of shock but luckily no bones broken. She had been cycling home from the village where she had gone to buy bottles of fizzy drink.

Kerstin has now filled me in on the background details.

She had agreed to cycle to Thorpe and buy some bottles of Corona for the rest of us. I don't remember but maybe she and the twins were doing something. On the way home, with several bottles in her basket, she skidded on some manure straight into a motorcyclist. Kerstin, broken bottles and glass everywhere. The bicycle was a complete write off but luckily Kerstin was not badly hurt and the ambulance was not called, even though the motorcyclist had cut his hands on the glass.

These days, the road or perhaps cart track, leading to Landermere off the main road from Thorpe-le-Soken to Frinton, Clacton and Walton has been closed off to the general public by a gate. Cailey went to visit once and discovered that Gull Cottages and the King's Head were unchanged. I think there was less left of the jetty though, the winds and tides of time had done their work on what remained of it in the early 1950's.

THE KING'S HEAD

GULL COTTAGES

LANDERMERE

THE HARD

KLARES AT FRINTON

STONELANDS

For the last year of my school life we lived at Stonelands in Sussex. Lucy Francis had moved her school there from Sible Hedingham and Klares got a job teaching weaving to the children. Bertie took the train to London every day, a shorter journey than the one from Landermere.

Two of Bertrand Russell's granddaughters, Sarah and Lucy were boarding at Stonelands at the time and Bertrand Russell came to tea one afternoon with his much younger wife. He was quite old and frail but he still had views on education, no doubt appreciating Lucy's more liberal approach.

I attended East Grinstead Grammar school and took my O levels. Kerstin was sent to Badminton school in Bristol and there was some talk of sending me to a cramming school but that did not eventuate, luckily!

Foxy had to be given away to some friends of Nell's as Sally, Lucy's daughter, had an Alsation dog and a couple of Labradors. Foxy would have been mincemeat if they got hold of him. I was not happy at my new school and after the first year, I told my parents I would not go back. They were upset but then Klares came up with the bright idea of Art School. She had always wanted to go to art school herself but her parents had insisted on her going to teachers training college. They wanted her to get a proper job.

In Klares' case, after two years of college, she went to England to do a year of practise training at Summerhill. Here she met A. S. Neil and when the year was up she never returned to live in Stockholm. Later she met Bertie and married and settled in England. Which just goes to show how things can end up being for the best.

In my case, starting at Brighton College of Arts enabled me later on to move to Sweden and enrol at Konstfackskolan in Stockholm to become an Interior Designer. This would not have happened if I had remained at school in Colchester and done my A levels and gone on to university.

Life at Stonelands was quite different to family life in Landermere. The staff was quite varied and a bit different from the usual run of teachers. One of them, Hans, was gay and had escaped with his Jewish parents from Germany to South Africa some time before the Second World War. His father had sold all his assets, bought gold and had it made into a gold bangle for his wife. The Nazis thought it was a bit of cheap costume jewelry and didn't bother to confiscate it.

A German woman on the staff, Hannah, compared everything in England unfavourably with all things German.

"In Germany we always did this…" invariably, of course, the German way was better. No one had the heart to mention the war!

On Sundays the teachers had to take it in turns to cook supper. Hans was always inventive. Once he made a shepherds pie, heavily spiced and garnished with sliced pineapple. Everyone tucked in and then Lucy suddenly said: "But Hans, where did you find the meat? There was no meat left after lunch."

Hans airily waved a hand "There were a whole lot of tins of Lassie in the larder, I used those!"

People suddenly lost their appetites and Sally was annoyed that all the dog food had been eaten.

We returned to Landermere for the holidays. I was always very sad when we drove along the track leading to the cottages and no little corgi came running out to greet us. He had always known the sound of our car, likewise Howie with the Hutton's car.

The highlight of my life at Stonelands was my first skiing holiday. Bertie suggested that we should ask Sally Francis and Gillian Spence to go with me. I was sixteen, Gillian a year or so older and Sally was in her twenties. Needless to say, the other two were keen on the idea.

We set off from Waterloo station on Boxing Day, equipped with all necessary clothing but minus skis and boots. Those would be hired when we got there. We crossed the Channel by ferry to somewhere in Belgium and continued by train to Mayerhofen. Mayerhofen is in the Tyrol, on the Austrian/German border with a view of the Zugspitze, a famous mountain top, in the distance.

We found ourselves in a picturesque snow covered village being greeted with *'Gruss gott!'* by all the natives. A representative of the travel agency met us and took us to our hotel. The three of us were in the same room and after getting rid of our luggage, we hurried downstairs to find where to go to hire boots and skis. The atmosphere was warm and cheerful and everything smelt of garlic; garlic was not very common in England at that time.

Next morning, bright sunshine, cold crisp air and time to line up on the beginners slopes, skis attached to our feet, poles at the ready. Everyone had to do a practise run down a gentle incline in order to be put into the correct class. Luckily we all ended up in the same beginners' class, under the tutelage of Hans, tall, blond, sunburnt and a good skier.

Hans took a shine to Sally and would come and call out to her under our window in the mornings, "Sally, shall I wax your skis?"

"Can you do mine too?" I stuck my head out beside Sally's.

"And mine?" Gillian wasn't going to be left out.

Good naturedly, Hans waxed all our skis and proved to be a good teacher as we all found ourselves snow ploughing, turning, stopping and traversing slopes, weight on the lower ski, upper shoulder forward, after the first week.

"Bend zee knees, my lady please!" Was a catch phrase on the ski runs.

I don't know what was said to the men. The handsome ski instructors probably weren't watching them so closely.

In the evenings there was dancing in various restaurants and the ski instructors all turned out to help entertain us. I took a fancy to one of them called Walter, dark haired, ruddy cheeked but he didn't speak much English. We danced together a few times and that was all there was to it.

We teased Sally about Hans and they teased me about Walter. "Walter, Walter, lead me to the altar!"

I started eating raw garlic, as that seemed to be the local custom. Gillian became friendly with an Englishman, a Cambridge undergraduate, so her holiday romance lasted a bit longer than ours but that fizzled out too in the end.

We spent three glorious weeks in Austria and all too soon it was time to make the journey home. The boat crossing was a bit rough and Gillian was seasick. I have never seen anyone turn such a

HANS WITH HIS CLASS

MAIDEN VOYAGE OF THE OSPREY

GILLIAN & SALLY

delicate shade of pale green before! We were reunited with our parents at Waterloo Station.

Bertie bent forward to kiss me and recoiled in horror "You stink of garlic!"

"Everyone eats garlic in Austria!" I replied defensively.

The holiday in Austria made me very dissatisfied with life in England. I was now at art school but I started thinking about becoming an au pair in France or some other European country. My parents were not keen on the idea. They pointed out all the disadvantages of looking after small children in a foreign country and all the advantages of carrying on with my studies, leading to a proper career.

Finally we all agreed on the perfect alternative: apply to study Interior Design in Stockholm at the art school there. I would have to go to evening classes and get a daytime job to support myself but that did not turn out to be a problem.

Klares wrote to her sister Viveka to ask if I could live with her and Nils in Djursholm and Basil Spence helped me to get a job with Astrid Sampe, a leading Swedish textile designer who ran her studio under the auspices of NK, a well known department store, in Stockholm. He also helped me to put my portfolio together for my application to get accepted into the Furniture and Interior Design course at Konstfackskolan.

KERSTIN, CENTRE, AT BADMINTON

FURTHER EDUCATION IN STOCKHOLM

I started evening classes at Konstfackskolan in September 1957. During the day I worked in NK's textile design studio, NKs *Textilkammare*, for Astrid Sampe.

I was living with my aunt Viveka and cousin Nils in Djursholm, a suburb lying to the North of the city. A light rail train took commuters to Engelbrecktsplan, practically in the middle of town. After many years, the local residents who had complained about the noise for many years, had their way. The train now stops at Östra station, next to KTH, the Royal Technical college.

Life in Astrid Sampe's studio was exciting and rewarding. Marianne Nilsson was chief designer and she had her own small *atelje* next door to the main studio. I had my drawing board in the main studio together with the secretary and Astrid had her studio cum office next to us. She would arrive with a flurry of notes which she handed round, flowers to be put into water and a strong whiff of scent.

Astrid was in her fifties, blond, petite with startling blue eyes, blue eye shadow to match and a perfume she sprayed about liberally. The eyelashes would flutter at whoever she was trying to impress and she was incredibly successful. She was an excellent business woman and she had a good eye for design. She put together textile design collections using designs from well-known architects and designers, Viola Grasten, Sven Markelius, Inez Svensson and Marianne Nilsson.

When I started she was in the middle of putting together a collection of fabric designs for the kitchen, *Linnelinjen*, Linen line. I had a minor part in the design of one of the iconic tea towels, *Perssons kryddskåp* or Persson's spice cupboard in English. It was revived again in 2010 and is still being sold at NK.

On one memorable occasion, an important client was not charmed by Astrid's batting eyelashes. Gio Ponti had designed the new Italian cultural centre for Stockholm. He visited Stockholm to inspect work in progress and Astrid had arranged for him to come to the studio with a view to landing the job of furnishing the new building.

We spent a few days arranging samples, tidying up and generally getting things organised to create a good impression on the great man. The day arrived, the suspense was palpable, everyone was hovering at their drawing boards, anxious to get a glimpse of the famous architect.

A flurry of men, with Gio Ponti in their midst, appeared in the doorway. Astrid billowed forth, hand outstretched to welcome him.

"What can I do for you?" was his gruff greeting.

" Oh no, it is we who would like to do something for you!" cooed Astrid in her most dulcet tones.

The group disappeared into Astrid's office and we all realised that Gio Ponti would be doing his own interior design scheme for the Italian cultural centre.

I worked in the textile design studio for a year and then I transferred to another department at NK where they sold contemporary furniture and fabrics. Lena Larsson, a well-known interior designer, had some involvement and we advised people on colours and choice of furniture. At the time, her motto was *slit och släng!* Wear out and throw out! Not such a popular sentiment today with everyone's awareness of saving the planet.

An interesting aside, Greta Garbo once worked at NK and it was here she was discovered, selling perfume. NK can take credit for having launched a number of careers, maybe not all quite so illustrious.

Konstfackskolan was close by, at Mäster Samuelsgatan but this area of Stockholm was scheduled for demolition and redevelopment. The developers were anxious to get their hands on Gamla Stan as well but luckily public outcry at this sacrilege prevented them.

By the autumn term of 1959 the new buildings for Konstfackskolan were completed on Valhallavägen, close to the open pastures at Gärdet, on the outskirts of town. The new premises were very modern and purpose built for teaching in all the design faculties. Each department had its own studios.

Interior designers had individual drawing tables with an adjacent plan cabinet for storing drawings. There was also a room with a large table and an area for tea and coffee making where the students in the two final years could get together and relax or maybe discuss future fundraising projects like what to make for the Christmas market or the dance we organised once a year. All profits went towards our study tour, which took us to Denmark one year, Finland the next.

During my final two years at Konstfack, in the higher degree course known as HKS , I had to study full time as there were no evening classes. I was able to obtain a study grant from the Swedish Government and with some financial support from Bertie, I managed. Besides this, I had been able to save some money during my previous year of employment with Ralph Alton, an interior designer who had his offices on Kungsholmen and who paid me a more generous salary than the one I had received at NK.

Suddenly I had some free time! Previously I had worked from nine till five and then attended classes from six till nine pm. On Saturdays I worked till midday and then went to a class from two till five. On Sundays there was usually homework, interior design projects mostly.

All my class mates had been in the same boat, which created a bond. For three years my social activities had involved either having dinner with some of them on a Saturday night at some cheap and cheerful pub, or going to a supper dance with Anita Nykänen (nee Helenius) and Birgitta Mjöman, (nee Granlund).

Students at HKS had a study trip each year. In order to raise money, each faculty was allowed to organise a dance and the profit from the dance plus income from the Christmas market, paid most of the travel expenses.

Our most successful trip was the one we made to Helsinki. We took the boat to Åbo and then train to Helsinki where we arrived at nine pm. Kaj Frank, head of the interior design faculty at the Atheneum and students from the course were there to meet us. Kaj Frank was very upset that they had not organised a welcome party but they made up for that over the next three days.

During the day we visited various factories, Ittala where they made glass and china. Kaj Frank was one of their designers and Artek. Artek, the furniture manufacturer that produces all of the Alvar Aalto iconic furniture designs.

We also looked at a number of buildings designed by Aalto and managed to fill all the daylight hours with useful study before being taken off to parties and dances by our Finnish hosts. I don't think I have ever spent such an interesting, entertaining or action packed three days in my life before or since. The Finnish visit definitely influenced my decision to go and work in Helsinki when I finished my course at HKS.

Back in Stockholm, we now had to concentrate on our major project for the degree in furniture and interior design. I got in touch with Jan Walinder, a second cousin who had an architectural practice in Gothenburg and asked him if he had a project I could do an interior design scheme for. He very kindly sent me the drawings for a library he had designed for the city of Jönköping. I set about producing an interior design scheme for the children's area: all the furniture layouts, special furniture design, the colour scheme and specifications and costs.

I successfully completed the course, graduating from HKS in 1962 and I was ready to tackle my first job as a qualified Interior Design Architect. I had applied and obtained a job at Stockmanns, a large department store in Helsinki, equivalent to NK in Stockholm. A new phase of my life was about to start.

KA ON RIGHT AT HKS

ASTRID SAMPE

PERSSONS KRYDDSKÅP

KA ON RIGHT WITH CLASSMATES

FINLAND

My first job, after I completed my studies at *Högre Konstindustriella Skolan*, HKS, in Stockholm in 1962, was at a prestigious department store in Helsinki, Stockmanns. I had had various student jobs while I was studying, working for different interior designers in Stockholm and also for Astrid Sampe, an innovative, trail-blazing textile designer.

In the 1960s you could walk in and out of jobs more or less as you pleased. When I wrote to Stockmanns, asking for employment and describing my qualifications, I was taken on without even an interview.

Stig Sallamaa was head of the interior design department and on my first day I was introduced to Greta Nordman. Thin, elderly, rather aristocratic-looking with short white hair and a long white draughting coat to protect her clothing.

"Welcome to Stockmanns!" She greeted me rather graciously. Her mother had been English , her father a Finnish-Swede and she was one of the first women to graduate in interior design from The Atheneum art college. She enunciated her words very precisely and enjoyed speaking English but we spoke mostly Swedish.

Finnish was the main language but Stockmanns was a Finnish-Swedish company and most of the staff spoke Swedish. I tried to learn Finnish in the beginning but gave up after a few lessons as the grammar was impossible. No prepositions and fifteen cases. Worse than Latin I decided.

Peini hetkännen, just a moment and *hänelle en ole tääla*, he or she isnt here, got me by on the phone and a few other standard phrases like *minna en ymmera*, I don't understand, stood me in good stead.

It was a perfect summer, as far as I remember. I stayed with a friend, Anita, who had studied in Stockholm with me and who was now married. Her husband, Paavo, was a surveyor and spent the summer working in the north of Finland. The days were more or less 24 hours long, north of the polar circle. You don't do much surveying there in the winter, when the land is envelopped in 24 hours of darkness and the ground is covered in metres thick snow.

The work was fun, designing showcases and built-in fittings for different departments or a new fit-out for a store they were opening up in the suburbs. Apart from Greta and Stig, I worked with two young male recent graduates, Pentii and Olavi. We got on well together and I made friends with a number of colleagues working in other departments.

I found Finnish people very open and friendly, despite their horrific experiences fighting against Russia in the Second World War. The Finns won the first round in 1940, the Winter War, thanks to their skiing prowess. Dressed in white, slipping between the trees, Mannerheim's men had the Russians on the run. Sadly, in their next encounter, the Russians won, due to sheer force of numbers. The Finnish population, only 4 million, was reduced to 3; they lost a large chunk of land, Karelia, and had to put up with a Russian occupying force along their south coast till the early 1960s. Finland was the only country which repaid its war debt.

At the weekends I visited some of my new friends in their country cottages, always in the depth of a forest, beside a lake with the obligatory sauna and dip in the icy waters to round off the day. Nice! Log fires burned in the open fireplaces and there was always fish and potatoes in some form or other on the menu.

One Saturday Anita and I took the train north to Rovaniemi to spend a week with Paavo, driving round and camping out in the Finnish tundra. Trees were not very tall in this neck of the woods, scarcely taller than a man. You completely lost track of time when the sun scarcely dipped below the horizon. At 10 o'clock at night, small children were out on the country lanes, herding a few reindeer.

We played cards in the evenings, no extra illumination required. Part of our travels took us to Inaari träsk, a sort of marshland close to the borders of Norway and Sweden. This was Lapp country and we saw a few Lapps dressed in traditional costume, navy blue with red and yellow trimmings. At one point we crossed the border into Norway. A small stream in a valley divided the two countries but what a world of difference in the landscape! The Norwegian side was much greener and Norwegian pine trees grew to spectacular heights.

"Must be the Gulf Stream," thought Paavo.

Paavo returned to Helsinki in September and I found lodgings for myself in the centre of town, just behind the Senate Square. It was 10 minutes walk from Stockmanns. Estnäsgatan 12 B was owned by an elderly spinster, fröken Spåre. She rented out three rooms in her rather spacious, once grand appartment to young women. I had to aquire some basic items of furniture, a bed a shelving unit, a table and some chairs. The lodgers shared the kitchen and bathroom with a separate lavatory. If you didn't like the loo paper fröken Spåre provided, torn up squares of *Hufvudstads Bladet*, you supplied your own.

I met an Irish girl called Dymphna Foley at a talk I attended at the Brittish Council and we started doing things together. She was working as an au pair for an English family but had most evenings off. We joined a Finnish-Swedish folk dancing group and got to see a bit more of the surrounding countryside as the folk dancing groups were constantly converging on some village or other and showing off their skills.

That winter, a particularly cold one with cutting winds straight off the steps of Siberia, was the year of the big strike. Public transport, all buses and trains were involved. Only the train to Lenningrad left Central station every day on time.

The ice breakers were also on strike which meant there were no ferries running between Helsinki and Stockholm. Some mad Scandinavian petrol heads decided to drive across the frozen Baltic Sea. Thankfully they arrived safely at their destination. The mere thought of all that black, chilly water, separated only by a layer of ice of variable thickness underneath their tyres, sent shivers down my spine!

There were plenty of opportunities for skiing. A favourite destination was across the bay from Helsinki to Tappiola, a modern sattelite town which included student residences. A large student self-service café was a good spot for lunch. Usually ham and pea soup followed by pancakes. On our way across we skied past a hole in the ice kept open for dedicated sauna bathers. After building up a good head of steam they would pad across the ice in their bathrobes to throw themselves in. You never saw a skinny person indulging in this activity and I was always glad I was well rugged up.

We took a different route skiing back to town, through a forest. There was a small ski-jump on the way, well patronised by local children who didn't look more than 8 or 10 years old. It was like a giant slide with steps up at one end so they had to carry their skis up, strap them on and hurtle down.

That Christmas I decided to go to London where my parents had recently moved into a flat in Great Ormond Street, opposite the famous children's hospital. Klares had written glowing reports of the joys of living so close to the City, just round the corner from The British Museum. For the first time in his life my father was able to walk to work, at the Treasury Solicitor's

ANITA & PAAVO

KA & ANITA'S MOTHER

ANITA & PAAVO

DYMPHNA

offices in Chancery Lane.

I caught the ferry from Helsinki to Stockholm, the strike had not yet started and spent the night with my aunt Viveka before flying to London. These days there is a direct flight to London from Helsinki. The flat in Great Ormond Street was full of character and charm. It was in a long row of 5 storey terrace houses, built in the 1600s. My parents had the top floor flat with a view out over rooftops and chimneys.

Christmas, as always in those long ago days, was magic. The weather was cold and every now and then one of the famous London pea-soupers, otherwise known as fogs, could bring the city to a standstill but the lights of Oxford and Regent Street dispelled the gloom and indoors it was always warm and cosy.

My godmother, Dodo White, who lived with her husband Eric in Cannonbury, invited us over for Christmas dinner. Dodo came from the north of England and her Christmas dinners were always very traditionally English, roast turkey or sometimes goose, roast potatoes, parsnips, beans, broccoli and gravy followed by plum pudding containing silver thruppences and sixpences. Holly, ivy and mistletoe decked the banisters and architraves and framed the scene after dinner as we drank coffee and exchanged Christmas presents.

A few days later we went to one of the theatres in Shaftesbury Avenue and saw the 'Way of the World' by Congreve, with a young Judy Dench and her then husband playing the main parts. It was a memorable Christmas and well worth the effort to get there.

Back in Finland, I resumed my work and my social activities. January always seemed to be a long month. Luckily, in those days there was always snow to lighten up the darkness. The stars did their best, glittering away in the far off galaxy and occasionally one was treated to a display of the aurora borealis. The sky streaked with spectacular rays of light, a myriad of colours all emanating from the North Pole.

I only had a few months left to work in Finland. Anita, Paavo and I thought that we would go to Leningrad for Easter and I wanted to spend one more Mid-summer and cray fish season in the north. After that I would return to England and take up an interior design position in the offices of Sir Basil Spence, Bonnington and Collins in Fitzroy Square in London.

LENINGRAD

Anita, Paavo and I decided that a trip to Leningrad, now St Petersburg, at Easter would be a nice thing to do. Something to look forward to. One could always count on the train running, thanks to Russian influence, and the journey would only take a few hours. We made the reservations, part of a group but that was the only way to get behind the iron curtain.

Easter fell early in April that year. It was still cold but the days were getting longer, the sun was getting warmer and things were looking more optimistic. We still wore warm winter overcoats and fur lined boots as we boarded the Leningrad Express, not quite up to the standards of the Orient Express but the thought of actually crossing the Russian border raised my feelings of excitement and expectation. A feature of the train was the samovar, located at the end of each corridor, together with an elderly Russian peasant to serve tea to whoever came and asked for a glass.

We rattled through the Finnish countryside, green fields, neat farms, and cattle grazing. All very idyllic and a complete contrast to what met our gaze as soon as we crossed the border, heavily fortified with barbed wire and concrete bunkers. We were still in Karelia, once part of Finland but now part of the USSR. There was no doubt that the land had suffered a very different fate to its prosperous neighbour. Nothing looked cared for and when we stopped in Viborg, once the fashionable capital of Karelia, it looked as though the war had only ended recently. Soldiers goose-stepped along the street, which was full of craters and there were bullet holes in the sides of the buildings. A peculiar scent or odour permeated the air as soon as you stepped out of the train and remained until you left the country. Moscow nights I called it.

The train only stopped for an hour in Viborg, before continuing on its way to Leningrad. We stayed at the Leningradskaja, an impressively grand hotel on one of the main squares, leading off the Nevski Prospekt. It was opposite the hotel Astoria where Hitler had planned to hold his victory celebrations.

There was snow on the ground, which probably enhanced the city, giving it a moderately clean appearance. Kindergarten children, wrapped up in so many layers of clothing they looked like little snowballs, made their way along the Boulevards attached to each other with rope, like mountaineers.

Unlike Viborg, restoration work had been carried out on a number of the buildings in Leningrad and its surroundings. We had a trip to Tsarskeseloe; a palace built by Catherine the Great, which had suffered all kinds of depredations under the occupying Nazi forces. However, the parts we were shown looked very grand and had obviously had a great deal of care and money spent on them to restore them to their former glory, even to the extent of gilding the main dome.

Walking around the grounds I was reminded of Russian fairy tales. There was a lake surrounded by pine trees with onion shaped domes in the distance. This was a perfect setting for Baba Yar, the infamous witch to come sweeping down on her broomstick. Or preferably, a handsome young prince might come riding up on his white charger. This didn't happen however.

On our second day we visited The Hermitage, The Winter Palace of the Tsars of Russia. The building itself was richly decorated with columns of lapis lazuli and onyx and various types of marble providing a backdrop for the fabulous art works. Catherine the Great had managed to amass quite a sizeable collection which had been added to over the years. The works by the Impressionists and Picasso were obviously a later additrion.

That evening we were allowed to spend the evening doing whatever we liked.

"How about dinner at the Astoria?"

I don't know who made the suggestion but we all thought it was a good idea.

The main dining room at the Astoria was indeed grand and not only dinner was being served but there was music and dancing as well. A waiter showed us to a table, whisked the cloth off and gave it a shake before we sat down. The menu must have been in English as Paavo ordered Wiener Schnitzel. I don't remember what I ordered, some Russian specialty perhaps. Paavo's schnitzels appeared, looking like two identical pieces of crumbed meat. However, one of them turned out to be fish but he made the best of it.

I had read in a guide to Russian customs that when a man took a woman to a restaurant, he would ask a woman from another table to dance, after first seeking permission from the other woman's escort. We watched some of the other couples and sure enough, this seemed to be the case. Rather unusual we thought. I was invited to dance several times by a young man who

LENINGRAD IN SUMMER

KIROV THEATRE

spoke very little English so we concentrated on dancing and smiling at each other.

When we were leaving and were just outside the dining room, I discovered I had left my gloves behind. I tried to go back but the doorman wouldn't let me in. Then my dance partner came to my rescue. I somehow managed to explain what had happened and he escorted me back to the table to retrieve my property. Women were not allowed unaccompanied into a restaurant, obviously.

On our last evening we visited the Kirov Theatre, now the Mariensky, a lovely sugar plum fairy type of building with turquoise and silver the main colour scheme. They were performing an opera of the founding of Leningrad. I don't know who wrote it but it has never been performed outside Russia to my knowledge. Before the overture we were treated to a long harangue. Goodness knows what it was all about as it was all in Russian.

The opera itself was curious. At one point the flooding of the Neva River was depicted, quite cleverly done with swathes of voile flapping like waves. In the interval all the opera patrons promenaded round the foyers and lobbies. This was another custom I had read about. Everyone promenaded round in order to see and be seen.

Next morning we were picked up by bus to take us to the railway station, together with the rest of our group.

Our guide got on the bus, "Someone has left a shirt in the hotel bedroom."

"That's okay." A young man responded, "they can have it."

"No they can't. Would you mind collecting it."

We had to wait while the youth collected the offending shirt.

A further hold up took place when the train reached the border. The border guards accused one of the Finnish men of not having the overcoat with him he had worn when he had entered the country. What an incredible memory, there must have been several hundred people on the train. The man protested his innocence and there we sat for a couple of hours. Finally the train set off again but I never found out if the guards had finally given up or the accused man had given in.

WINE MAKING

Klares' wine making career started when we lived in Landermere, sometime in the early 1950s. She and Nell Hutton used to produce a wine made from potatoes, a potent drop! An elderly friend, Greba Pilkington, came to dinner once. The home made wine was served but after half a glass, Greba suddenly got up and went outside. After a few minutes we followed her and found her stretched out on the garden path, gazing up at the night sky, giggling.

"The stars are so pretty, I just had to lie down and look at them."

Klares and Bertie moved to London in 1962, to a top floor flat at 57 Great Ormond Street. This was a 17th century building owned by SPAB, The Society for the Protection of Ancient Buildings. It was a lovely old flat with two bedrooms, a sitting room, dining room, kitchen and bathroom. No two walls were parallel and neither was anything at right angles to anything else but that added to the charm. It was opposite the famous children's hospital in the depths of Bloomsbury.

For once in his life, Bertie could walk to work at the Treasury Solicitor's office in Chancery Lane. Kerstin and I lived with them for a couple of years and I too could walk to my work in Fitzroy Gardens, where I worked as an interior designer for Spence, Bonnington and Collins.

Klares had done a lot of weaving in the country but she got rid of her loom when they moved to London. She now needed some new activity to devote herself to. A local adult education group had its headquarters in Queen's Square, at one end of Great Ormond Street. She went in one day to see what courses they were offering and discovered that wine making was one of them. That sounded promising. She and Nell had made wine in Landermere but now she could learn how to do it properly.

"You should come too. I expect the other students will be interesting."

It was an evening class so I was easily persuaded.

The man who ran the class was elderly, slightly over weight who we christened Joe Bananas as he usually suggested throwing a few banana skins into the brew. Maybe they were rich in yeast? His wife was quite the opposite, small and slight. Not surprising as she never seemed to ingest anything other than alcohol and cigarette smoke.

We soon got the hang of producing wine and in no time there were several demijohns fitted with airlocks bubbling away in the kitchen. Raisins created the fermentation and rice or parsley or elderflowers added the *je ne sais quoi*. Every week we met up with the class to sample a particular wine from Joe's ample cellar, compare notes and seek advice.

"Throw in some banana skins," seemed to solve many of the problems, especially if things had got stuck mid process.

Every now and then one had to siphon the liquid off the lees, a rather muddy looking substance that remained on the bottom of the demijohn. The demijohn was washed and a specific gravity reading to test the alcohol level was taken before returning the wine to the demijohn to carry on with its activity. Finally, when it stopped bubbling and the wine was clear, it was ready to bottle. We tried to keep the odd bottle to mature but most of it was drunk soon after production.

Nell Hutton, who now lived in Cambridge, took to wine making like a duck to water. She and Klares swapped hints and recipes for the next twenty years. Elderflower wine was a popular drop but my favourite was parsley wine. This was a beautiful clear liquid with a greenish tinge. Not too sweet, not too dry. Goldilocks would have approved.

As Klares had suspected, the other students were interesting. One of them, Louise, lived in a top floor flat in Lamb's Conduit Street, just around the corner. The only drawback in my opinion was that there was an undertaker's establishment on the ground floor. Louise paid quite a low rent in exchange for every now and then showing grieving relatives their departed loved one. Once or twice she opened the wrong casket but that didn't seem to worry her too much.

Klares and I agreed that living there would give us nightmares, even if we paid no rent at all.

Another woman, Betty Wright, was an Australian. She had been married to an American and lived in Beirut for a number of years. Her previous husband's family, the Vesters, owned The American Colony Hotel in Jerusalem. Life in the Middle East sounded very exotic, interesting people and numerous parties. Betty had met the spies Burgess and Maclean there, before they defected to Moscow.

GREAT ORMOND STREET

GREAT ORMOND STREET INTERIOR

A third fellow student was a woman named Jean. A very matter-of-fact person, she lived with her husband and an Alsation dog. We didn't know at the time but Jean was suffering from cancer. Later, when she died, Klares went to the funeral. At the wake her husband handed round a plate of cakes.

"Jean made these six months ago," he informed the guests.

When Klares told me the story she said she was reminded of a joke from a Swedish cartoon. Cakes were being passed round at a wake and the guests were urged to take one with the words, " the corpse baked these herself."

After I married, Nicholas and I lived in a flat in Great James Street, just round the corner from Lambs Conduit Street, close to Great Ormond Street. I carried on making wine, assisted by Nicholas. He took it one step further and tried his hand at a bit of distilling. We had been given some distilling equipment by a chemist we met on a skiing trip in Austria. The results were not as successful as the wine though.

When we were preparing for our overland trip in 1968 it seemed like a good idea to include a few bottles of wine with our rations. Unfortunately we didn't get to drink it all as some of the bottles popped their corks in Morocco. We suddenly noticed a delicious aroma of wine as we were driving along past a small Moroccan village.

"There must be some illegal wine making going on," I laughed.

But then the horrible truth dawned. The smell of wine was emanating from the back of our camper van. Luckily not more than a couple of bottles but that was bad enough, given that most of the countries we were driving through did not sell wine and the locals were not allowed to drink alcohol.

Later, when we settled in Sydney, we decided to carry on making wine. We found a place that sold all the necessary equipment and we soon had a few demijohns bubbling away in the kitchen of our studio flat in Macleay Street in Potts Point. In those days it was legal to make wine but not beer.

One day the man, who had sold us the equipment, rang up, "the customs and excise men have been here and they have gone through my books. They are checking up on all my customers, whatever you do, don't make beer!"

Sure enough, a few days later two men knocked on our door. They were dressed in raincoats and fedoras and looked like a couple of detectives out of a Raymond Chandler film. They came in and demanded to search the premises but all they found were the demijohns, obviously in the process of producing wine. A quick glance round our single room convinced them that nothing illicit was happening and that was the last we heard of them.

We continued making wine for a few years but then house renovations and the birth of our son Alex took up all our spare time. I am not tempted to start making wine again, after all these years but I still remember going to a party with two bottles of my parsley wine and people queuing up for a glass.

KLARES

My mother, Klares, was christened Wendla Klares Arla Linder but called Klares. Her parents did not want her to have the initials KWAL which spells pain or agony in Swedish.

Her father, Ludvig Linder, was a head librarian at the *Kungliga Biblioteket* (Royal Library) in Stockholm and her mother, Selma Linder, was the last of the women in the family to stay at home and look after the household, after she married. Selma's father, Carl Jacob Rossander, had been a surgeon at the Karolinska hospital in Stockholm and personal physician to the Swedish queen Viktoria. Ludvig's father, Carl Wilhelm Linder, was the Dean, *Domprost* at Linköping cathedral when he died at the early age of 57.

Klares was the third daughter, her two older sisters were Barbro and Viveka and Ulla was the youngest. Klares was a bit of a rebel. She would have loved to go to art school but her parents wanted her to have a proper career like her sisters, who all went to university. Klares settled for teachers' training college.

The first family home in Stockholm was at Tyrgatan 9, a house designed by one of Klares' uncles who was an architect, Eric Hahr, in the National Romantic style. Her father had quite a bit of input and above the entrance door is a quote which he dictated.

This was one of Hahr's first projects and one of his last was a house he designed for Viveka and her husband Eric Granlund, Tyrvägen 18. Sadly Eric died before they moved in but Viveka and her son Nils have lived in the house ever since. Nils took over the house from his mother in the 1970's. Family fortunes rose and fell and the family had to sell the house at Tyrgatan and move to a flat on Karlbergsvägen 44. Or maybe they sold the house in order to buy an appartment block at Sibyllegatan 77, where the family moved in 1919, just after the First World War. They lived in one of the flats and the others were rented out.

Klares wrote a diary that year when she was 13. She presents a picture of life in a typical Swedish bourgeois family: get-togethers with aunts, uncles and cousins, trips to the weekend cottage, school friends and the odd mention of school.

On one occasion, she went with her father to pick up their sailing boat, which had been left over the winter with a fisherman in the archipelago at Möja. Sailing it back to their weekend cottage at Viggbyholm, they had the wind and the weather in their favour. They did the trip in seven hours which was apparently a record. This was mentioned in a memorial booklet about Ludvig but he had not said that Klares had been with him.

One summer, her parents were away and Klares was left in charge of looking after the household. She had decided she wanted to go to Paris so many of the meals she served up were a form of Yoghurt, *filmjölk,* in order to save up money for her trip. I asked my aunt Viveka about this once.

"Yes, and we nearly starved!" She had not forgotten.

After two years Klares had to do a years practical training and she decided to go to England and work at Summerhill, a progressive coeducational boarding school run by A. S. Neil. Klares may have found out about Summerhill through Barbro who was studying at Uppsala university or Viveka, who had become a Theosophist during her law studies. Later, Viveka was employed at the Historical Museum and after that the Nordiska Museum as their legal advisor.

For some reason, Selma decided it would be safer if she sewed Klares passport into her bra. As Klares stepped on board the boat she was asked to show her passport. She blushed with embarassment and shot down to her cabin to retrieve the vital document.

Klares spent a happy time at Summerhill and became friends with Neil and his wife, known as Mrs Lindsey and also Lucy Francis. Later on Lucy left and started up her own progressive school, Kingsmuir.

Neil had written several books on his system of education and Klares translated a number of them into Swedish. *Den Förskräcklige Skolan* (That Dreadful School) was one of them. She did not return to live in Stockholm after the year was up and at one point she did a course in London on cosmetics, run by Helena Rubinstein.

Klares did not seem to have any particular job during this period. She did some translating and later, when she married Bertie on 11th August 1934, they translated Swedish books into English. One of these, Land of Ice and Fire, was about one of the glaciers, Vatnajökull, on Iceland.

Selma died in 1939 and Klares took me over to Stockholm at Christmas to spend time with her father. The Second World War had already started but one of her cousins, Sven Lindeberg, was in the diplomatic corps and he was able to organise passage on a a flight for her.

By March the war was getting serious and to Ludvig's distress, Klares decided it was time to return to England. She had lost a silver necklace, a favourite of hers, while she was staying with her father.

"If you find the necklace, England will win the war!"

Needless to say, the necklace was found, stuffed down behind some cushions in a sofa and Viveka quickly wrote Klares a letter with the glad tidings. She was able to receive letters from her family during the war, all of them heavily censored.

Ludvig died in 1944 and Klares did not return to Stockholm till late in 1945, after the war had ended. She had Kerstin with her this time and at first they stayed in an hotel in Östermalm but later she went to stay with Viveka in Djursholm, Tyrvägen 18.

She got work at the local Swedish radio, giving talks on what it had been like, spending the war years in England and she took lessons in weaving. She and Nell Hutton were planning to set up a weaving studio at 43 Belsize Park Gardens and sell Swedish rag rugs to Heals. Heals was a shop in Tottenham Court Road, famous for its modern, Scandinavian design. Klares and Bertie had bought a coffee table there, designed by Bruno Mattsson, when they got married.

Back in London, after a lengthy absence, Klares and Nell acquired a couple of looms and were soon producing rag rugs which were snapped up by Heals as fast as they could weave them. I am not sure who proposed the idea of a book but Nell and Klares were soon busy writing their first book on how to weave rugs. The book was titled Your Rug Making and was published by the Sylvan Press in 1950. Later the book was translated into German.

After the move to Landermere the rug weaving continued. Bertie and John built a separate shed for the looms as the cottages were too cramped to house weaving and all the paraphernalia that went with it.

I don't know how happy she really was, living in the country. Klares had spent her childhood in Stockholm. She was used to having cinemas, theatres, museums and art galleries within easy reach but she never complained to Kerstin or me about her life. I think weaving and designing rugs gave her pleasure and allowed her creative talents to find an outlet.

She was a good swimmer, doing the Australian crawl, in between beautiful swallow dives off one of the posts that remained from the jetty at Landermere. I think she was probably the best swimmer among the adults.

After Landermere the family lived at Stonelands for three years where Klares taught weaving and experimented with tapestry weaving but that was hard on the eyes and she had to start wearing glasses.

The Huttons decided to leave Landermere and took a lease on a house in Nayland in Suffolk and asked Klares and Bertie to join them. I was living in Sweden by this stage and Kerstin had just finished her O-levels at Badminton and was ready to start on the next phase of her education. She and Wocky Hutton enrolled at the Colchester College of Art where one of their teachers was John Nash, brother to Paul.

Klares had now managed to channel both of her daughters into Art School, hopefully making up for her own disappointment in that regard!

The first book on weaving had been a success and now, ten years later, it seemed a good idea to write a second book. Wocky and I were commissioned to produce the illustrations. Klares had wanted our names included as illustrators but Nell vetoed this. Bertie wrote an appendix on how to build your own loom and he was not acknowledged either. This book was called Rug Weaving and was published in 1962 by B. T. Batsford Ltd.

Sharing a house with the Huttons came to an end when Nell and John separated and divorced in 1962 and Klares and Bertie moved to London, renting the flat in Great Ormond Street. Finally Klares was back living in a city, close to the British Museum which she loved to visit and not far from the National Gallery. When I was a child, Klares used to tempt me into the gallery to see Charles 1st on horseback. Later she used this method to tempt Alex in. They ran into one of the attendants and started talking.

"I'm going to see an old friend of my mother's," Alex told him.

"That's nice"

"On horseback."

The attendant looked suitably bemused.

Now they were living in London, Klares enrolled in the jewellery classes at the John Cass. She also did some enamelling and it was not long before the idea of writing a book on the subject struck her. She got a contract with Batsford, the company who had published the last book on weaving and got stuck into it. I was living at home again so I was asked to do the illustrations. Bertie helped with the editing and wrote some of the chapters but once more, he wanted no acknowledgement. Just as well, Klares felt too embarrassed to return to the jewellery classes, once the book was published.

Klares and Bertie moved to a terrace house they bought in 1968 in Blackheath, encouraged by Kerstin's husband John Hegarty. He was shocked to discover that they were still renting their accommodation. Their life at 13 Tristan Square was very happy. They made friends with a number of the neighbours, several of them who had children the same age as their grandchildren. The house was large enough for family to come and stay, at times bursting at the seams. Bertie died in 1978 and in 1982 Klares moved to Oxford to be near Kerstin. At first she lived in Kerstin's garage, which had been converted into a very comfortable cottage with central heating and a spare bedroom in the attic. I stayed there one summer but when I visited in the winter I stayed with Kerstin, the attic was too cold.

In 1987 Klares moved into a flat in a retirement village near Oxford, Parklands and Kerstin moved into a house in Oxford. Kerstin was managing all Klares' affairs by now. She visited her constantly, took her shopping and provided all the important support. Klares became good friends with her neighbour, Elizabeth Hamilton, who later married one of the retired men living at Parklands, Peter Goozee.

After Bertie died, Klares made a number of visits to Australia. Alex and I both loved having her to stay with us and it was always a sad moment when it was time to drive her to the airport to leave. Sometimes though, we would all leave together. Kerstin was always there at Heathrow to meet us and Alex grew up feeling very much a part of his English family.

Klares died on the 29 December 2001. Kerstin was staying with me in Australia and we had phoned her up the night before to wish her a Happy New Year. I had always suspected that I might not be with her at the end but it was especially sad for Kerstin not to be there, as she and Klares had been so close, ever since Bertie died in 1978.

Their ashes are now together in a grave marked with a headstone in a corner in the graveyard next to the church at Cumnor near Oxford. A friendly gargoyle is keeping an eye on them.

BARBRO, VIVEKA, KLARES & ULLA

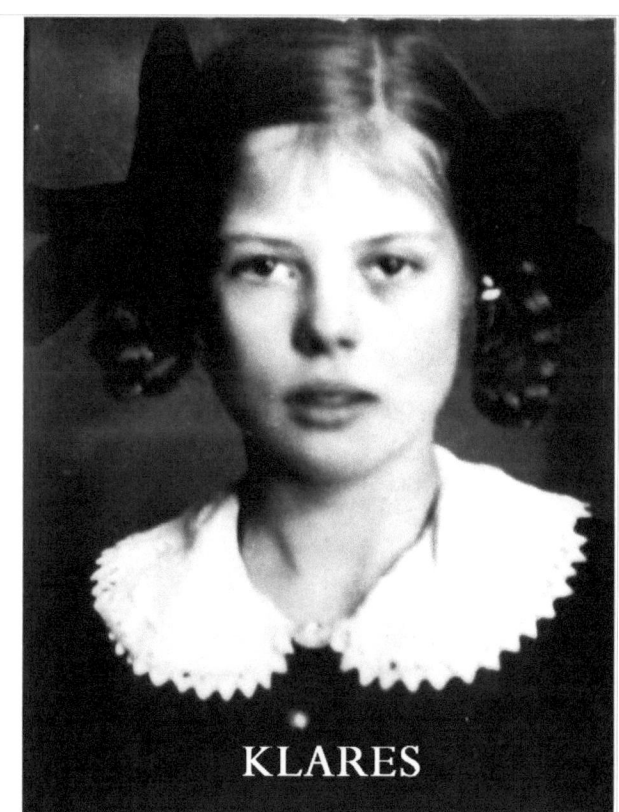

KLARES

KLARES AT LANDERMERE

BERTIE LEWES

My father, Bertie, was named Cyril Herbert Alfred Leung and he was born 2nd June 1908 in Berlin. His mother, Hedvig, was German and his father was from British Guiana (Now Guyana) in South America. This made him a British subject even though his father, my paternal great grandfather was Chinese and my great grandmother was a bit of a mixture, including South American Indian.

Bertie's older brother was called Francis after his father and at the outbreak of the First World War, in August 1914, he and Bertie were with their maternal grandparents in Berlin. Granny may have been with them. My Grandfather was a barrister and he had his practice in Secondee on the Gold Coast (now Ghana) in West Africa. Known as the white man's grave, Granny and her four boys only visited him during the cooler months of the year.

Foreigners were given 24 hours to leave Germany so Bertie, age six and eight year old Francis were taken by an aunt to spend the war in Neuchatel in Switzerland. They went by train with all the blinds pulled down so they couldn't spy on the Germans en route.

I think these were the happiest years of my father's childhood. He always spoke of his Aunt Elsa with great fondness. She was probably a gentler and warmer person than Granny, not having had the responsibilities of the eldest daughter with ten younger siblings. Sadly, she died in a concentration camp during the Second World War. Granny had a photograph of her in nurse's uniform, in her sitting room.

Several letters written to the boys in Switzerland by their father survive. In one, written in 1915, he describes the family Christmas and in another he thanks my uncle ' *for his first French letter.*'

They spent a carefree war in neutral Switzerland and their walk to school every day took them past a chocolate factory. Every now and then the local schoolchildren were given bags of broken chocolate. This was one of Bertie's happiest childhood memories.

The war ended and Granny arrived in Switzerland, almost a stranger to her sons after four years. Their father had died of yellow fever in 1916.

"I am your mother" she announced and without further ado carried them off back to London.

The boys were sent to Dulwich College, a respectable Public School and teased because of their foreign appearance and foreign accents. Granny hired a young man who came and read The Times with them to teach them English and improve their vocabulary. This obviously paid off because Bertie was able to study law at London University and become a Barrister. By the time he met Klares he had eaten the required number of lunches and been called to the Bar. He had also changed his surname to Lewes (after Lewes Assizes) in order to overcome any racial discrimination.

Early on in the Second World War, Klares and Bertie moved to Assington Hall. Not long after that, Bertie was called up, as were all the other men whose families were living there.

Bertie came home on leave from time to time. This was more difficult after we moved to Wales as train travel was slow, taking up most of the precious leave time. I can remember being very impressed with his uniform and the leather straps and shiny brass buttons. All of which had to be polished, though later on this work was carried out by his batman.

After a year in Wales, Klares and Nell moved to London. Belsize Park Gardens might have been easier to reach when the men were on leave but neither Bertie nor John Hutton thought it was very safe and couldn't wait to return to the front. I suppose they felt they had the enemy more under control there and could fight back. In London we were like sitting ducks and had to take shelter under the staircase when we heard the air raid sirens. Klares had noticed that staircases were usually left standing after a house had been bombed.

Bertie was in a tanks division and landed in Normandy on D Day plus 2. Shortly afterwards he got transferred to 30th corps, under Field Marshall Montgomery. This was thanks to one of his friends from Assington Hall, Bill Williams, who was working in Intelligence and knew that Bertie spoke fluent French and German. The transfer also saved his life. One week later, his tank unit was wiped out in a battle near Caen.

Not knowing any of this of course, Klares and I picked up on a popular song of the time…"*If it wasn't the tanks that won the war it was my boy Willie,*" which we changed to Bertie.

I loved going out for walks with Bertie in his uniform and seeing other soldiers salute him and he return the salute. Was it Mrs. Bennett in Pride and Prejudice who said something along the lines of, '*I am partial to a man in a nice uniform!*'

The War was the only life I had known at that stage and I couldn't really imagine what life would be like with no war. I hoped that at least we would not have to listen to the news any longer, full of boring information about fighting. There were posters everywhere showing two people on a park bench gossiping, with Hitler hiding under the bench or behind a wall with the caption, '*Careless talk costs lives!*'

When the War came to an end in 1945, I was at Kingsmuir boarding school and Bertie was then stationed with the occupying forces in Germany. As soon as she was allowed to travel, Klares went to Sweden to recover, taking Kerstin with her. She was able to get some work for the local radio in Stockholm, talking about her wartime experiences.

It was over a year before I saw Bertie again. He was waiting for me at the docks at Gothenburg when I arrived on the SS Suecia from Harwich. He was in uniform as he had just arrived from Germany. He bought me a large bag of sweets, sweets were strictly rationed in England and we boarded the train for Stockholm. Our carriage was full and everyone was very friendly. Neither Bertie or I spoke much Swedish but Bertie might have been able to speak to some of our fellow passengers in German. German was the first foreign language taught in Swedish schools before the Second World War.

I handed round my sweets and received bars of chocolate and fruit in return. All of which had been practically non-existent in England during the war. Sweden had luckily managed to remain neutral.

In 1948 Bertie was demobbed and we all returned to Belsize Park Gardens. Bertie decided not to return to private practice and got a job in the Treasury Solicitor's office. John Hutton had already given up law and devoted himself to art. Both families were now not so well off which dictated our next move, to the country.

Through friends, the Huttons discovered Landermere, a collection of coastguard cottages and a decommissioned pub on the shores of an estuary in Essex. These properties were owned by Karin Stephen, who had been married to Adrian Stephen, brother of Virginia Woolf.

Bertie had a two-hour journey up to London every day, returning again in the evening about 7 o'clock. Klares sometimes met him at the station and when the train was late she would repair to the pub to while away the time. Those train trips were not much fun during the winter, snow and fog often causing delays. John Hutton spent the week in London at his studio and only came down for weekends.

The Treasury Solicitor's office represented the Crown and the barristers spent a lot of time in prosecuting people for black market offences or some contravention of Government rules and regulations. Sometimes Bertie would have a case in another part of the country and then he might be away for a night or so. Once he came home with 100 pounds in his pocket, the fine paid for some misdeed. The cashier had closed for the day so Bertie had to take the money with him. We would have loved to be able to keep it, a small fortune in today's money!

One Christmas, when my parent's finances were at their lowest ebb, Granny sent us five pounds for presents. Klares, Kerstin and I cycled into Colchester and visited a second hand shop where we bought a guitar for Bertie and other things for the rest of us. The guitar was a great success. Bertie taught himself to play and John Hutton was also inspired to take it up. Andres Segovia was a favourite composer and every time I hear one of his pieces on the radio I can remember lying in bed at night, listening to John and Bertie practising as I drifted off to sleep.

Sailing was another popular pastime at Landermere. Karin Stephen was a keen sailor and she liked to rope in Bertie and the twins to come sailing with her. Klares was not very keen, even though she had done quite a bit of sailing in her childhood with her father in the Stockholm archipelago. Once, when they were getting ready to set off, Karin Stephen was barking out directives, Bertie was getting ready to hoist the sail and Klares was sitting in the stern knitting. Kerstin and I were preparing to shove the boat out to sea when a terrific gust of wind caught the sail half way up the mast and the boat keeled over, taking in a large amount of water. Klares sat there with her knitting, ankle deep in water, a look of complete surprise on her face. Kerstin and I couldn't stop laughing.

Another of Bertie's talents was tinkering with cars. Our first family car was a pre war Austin 7 and one Christmas Bertie, assisted by Wocky and Cailey, spent the festive season refurbishing the engine. Christmas dinner had to vie for space on the kitchen table with major vital parts of what was usually under the bonnet of the car.

Kerstin and I were not interested in mechanics but the twins never forgot this experience, one of the highlights of growing up in Landermere. Bertie gave them a lot of practical experience but their parents, John and Nell, passed on their artistic talents. Cailey became an architect and Wocky became an artist and an illustrator of children's books, some of which he wrote himself.

After Landermere we spent three years living at Stonelands, a boarding school run by Klares' old friend, Lucy Francis. Klares taught weaving to the children, I went to the local grammar school for a year and then spent two years at Brighton College of Art. Kerstin went to boarding school, Badminton, in Bristol. Bertie continued to travel up to London every day to work but the journey was much shorter than the one from Landermere, only one hour instead of two.

We returned to Landermere for the school holidays and Bertie, inspired by Basil Spence, decided to build a sailing boat. Basil had built a 505 for himself or possibly for his son John, from a kit, much to everyone's admiration.

Bertie had always been good at carpentry and the idea of building his own sailing boat was too tempting to resist and he sent off for a kit to build an Osprey. Living at Stonelands was ideal. There was a large ballroom there and Lucy kindly allowed him to take up part of the space for his boat building project.

The planks for the side of the boat had to be steamed so they could bend round the hull. Bertie set up an arrangement with metal downpipes and a boiling kettle on a small fire outside on the sloping lawn. Each plank was placed in the downpipe and arranged so that steam from the kettle was directed up the downpipe. After a while the planks would be pliable enough to attach to the hull. My job was to man the steaming process, keep the fire going and the kettle boiling.

By the time the Osprey was built, I had already left for Sweden but two of my cousins, Ann-Charlotte and Carl-Wilhelm Welin were in England, staying with Klares and Bertie at the time. Carl-Wilhelm still remembers driving with the boat on a trailer, accross the country to Essex. They were also able to take part in its maiden voyage. I never saw it in its final state myself.

During his time at Stonelands, Bertie decided to take up silver smithing and jewelry making. He took evening classes at the John Cass school in London and later on Klares joined him. I have many rings and other pieces of jewelry made for me by both of them. Also silver beakers, candle-sticks, a coffee pot and a sugar bowl made by Bertie He had his own hall mark and he always got the pieces registered with the current silver mark.

Later, when they were living at Great Ormond Street, Klares decided to write a book on jewelry making. She had already written a couple of books on rug weaving with Nell Hutton so she was able to get a contract with Batsford Press. She asked me to do the illustrations and Bertie helped her, both with the writing and editing but he did not want his name mentioned, possibly because he was still going to classes at the John Cass.

FRANCIS, FREDERICK, HAROLD & BERTIE

BERTIE

SILVERSMITHING

Bertie retired from the Treasury Solicitor's when he was 65. He took on a job as a Chairman of Industrial Tribunals, based in Ashford in Kent. As a civil judge he spent the last five years of his life happily employed in making judgments. He was involved in a high profile case concerning newspapers and printing and his name was in all the papers because for some reason he declined to judge.

A few weeks before he died I wrote to him and asked him what he would like for Christmas.

"Nothing," he wrote back, "I am the man who has everything!"

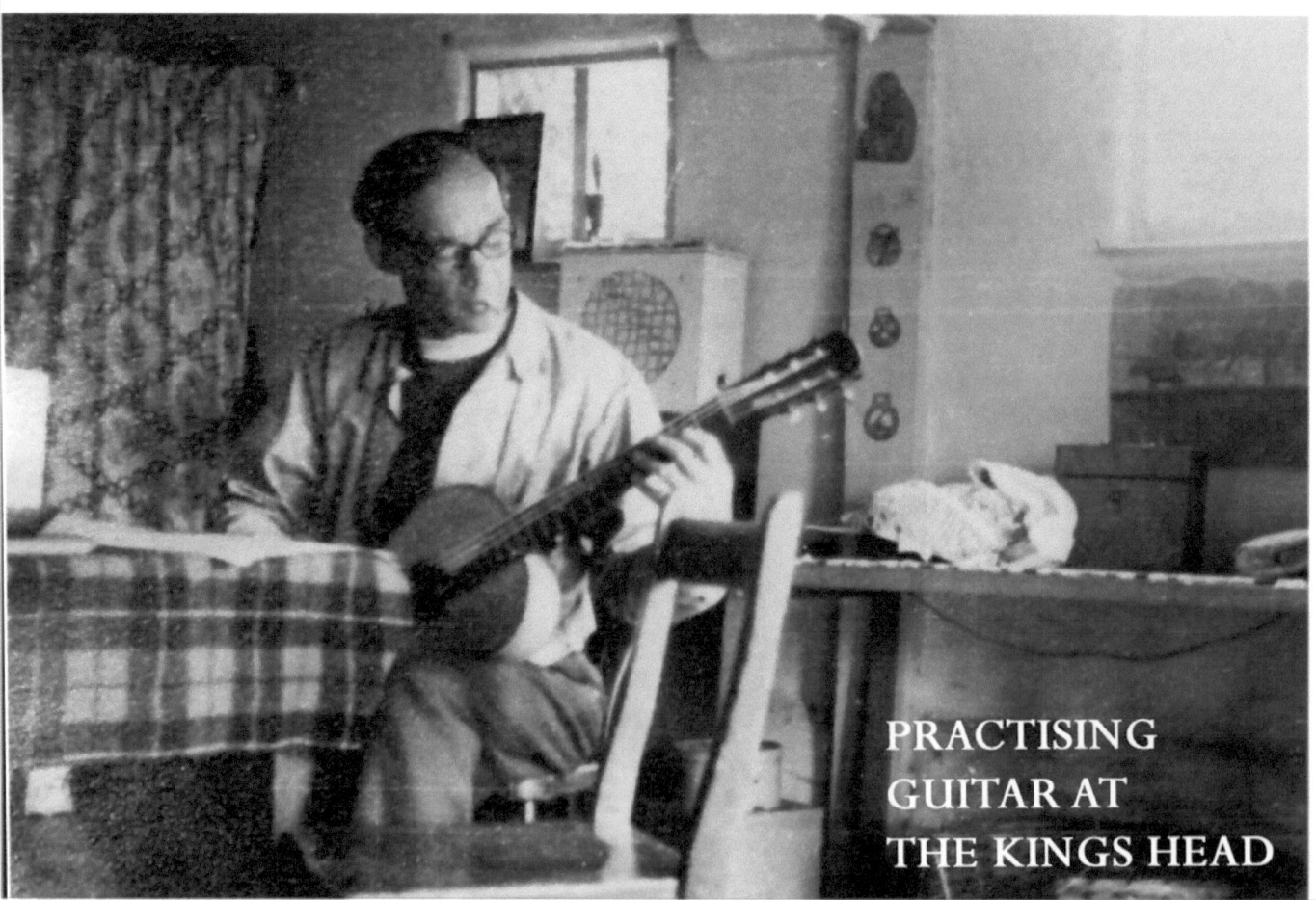

PRACTISING GUITAR AT THE KINGS HEAD

GRANNY

My paternal grandmother, Granny as she was known to us and all our friends, always seemed to me an old woman but she would only have been in her 60s when I first got to know her.

"Have you washed your hands?" or "How many elbows can I see on the table?" were two of her stock phrases that come to mind.

Born Hedwig Selma Weintraub in 1881, she came from Berlin. The eldest of 11 children, she couldn't wait to leave home and went first to Paris as an au pair to study French and then to London to learn English. There she met Grandfather, Francis Stanislaus Xavier Leung, of mixed South American and Chinese descent, from Georgetown, British Guiana. He had studied at London University and was a barrister-at-law.

They married in June 1904 in London. I can't imagine what her parents thought of their daughter marrying a man of multicultural descent, a Roman Catholic to boot. Her father was Jewish, her mother Lutheran and Hedwig herself a dissenter. Her four sons were all agnostics.

It is rumoured, in family circles, that she once met and chatted to Nietzsche but unfortunately I never asked her about her past and did not become interested till it was too late.

Her eldest son was named Francis after his father. Her second son, my father, was named Cyril Herbert Alfred and called Bertie by all his friends. Granny always called him Herbert with a strong German accent. The two younger boys were Fredrick and Harold.

My grandfather set up his practice in Seccondee (Sekondi) on the West African Gold Coast, now Ghana, known in those days as 'The White Man's Grave.' He was also a local puisne judge. Granny remained in London with her expanding family of boys and visited her husband during the cooler season of the year.

Another rumour from the family archives is that she was bored one afternoon and got her bearers to take her for a row down the river, possibly the Ankobra. An explorer, who had been in the jungle for some time, was returning to civilisation. He was amazed to see a boat being rowed by a couple of African men with a white woman seated in the stern, dressed in white with a large white parasol shading her face.

At the outbreak of World War One, my father and his older brother, then age six and eight, were staying with their grandparents in Berlin. All British citizens, children included, were given 24 hours to get out of the country. Their aunt Elsa took them by train to Neuchatel in Switzerland. The blinds in the carriages had to be drawn down and at one point the train was stoned. Luckily Switzerland has always managed to remain neutral.

I have a copy of a sweet letter Grandfather wrote to them in 1915, describing the antics of their baby brothers, who were there with Granny. Granny and the two youngest boys spent most of the war in London. They would still have been able to sail to West Africa, as there was not a major threat of U-boats and the west of France had not been captured by the Germans.

Granny, being German, was not well treated in England but she was not interred. Rations were short and she had to beg people for food sometimes but they survived. My father and uncle had a much better time in Switzerland, living near a chocolate factory which handed out free bags of broken chocolate to the local children.

In 1916 Grandfather died. It is said he died of yellow fever but cousin Martin once told me that he was threatened by a vigilante group for having married a German and he committed suicide. Maybe Granny told him this but I can hardly believe it. Not only did he have his wife to think of, he had four young boys who would be fatherless.

In 1918 Granny appeared in Neuchatel and took the two boys back to England. Life had been quite idyllic with their aunt so this was a shock, to Bertie at least. Now, aged 10, he scarcely remembered his mother and never forgave her.

Back in London, they were sent to Dulwich College and teased for their foreign appearance and not being able to speak English. Granny engaged a man to come and read The Times with them so eventually that hurdle was overcome and they both completed school and university, Francis became an engineer and Bertie a barrister.

As long as I remember, Granny lived in Twickenham in a semi-detached Edwardian house,

209 Richmond Road, opposite an entrance to Richmond Park. She had an allotment in the park and whenever the milkman's horse did his business on the road outside, she would nip out with a shovel to scoop it up and add it to her compost heap.

I don't think the local shopkeepers were very keen on her. We would be sent to buy bread with a cloth bag she had sewn for the purpose. The baker would give us a dirty look, pick up the bread in his hand and shove it into the bag. He was supposed not to touch it!

Granny meant well, always did her best and was a great support to her family in many ways. She looked after me during school holidays when Klares and Kerstin had gone to Sweden and Bertie was still with the army in Germany. She was also extremely generous. One Christmas, when the family was particularly short of funds, she sent Klares five pounds to buy us all Christmas presents, as I mentioned before.

When we were older, she liked to take Kerstin and me to tea at D.H.Evans and once she took us to the theatre in Richmond to see Lilac Time.

Her least appealing trait was that she was tactless to a degree. She managed to get all her daughters-in law off side.

Klares told me how Granny came to visit them in their new flat in Regent's Park Terrace in London. She inspected it without comment. The following week she said "I've been thinking and I know how you can make the place really nice!"

Another time Klares showed her a jumper she had just finished knitting for herself. Granny studied it closely and then announced "and there's a mistake!"

One of my aunts was a bit overweight and she observed "you sit there eating all day long, you will never lose weight!" Granny couldn't understand why that daughter-in-law went off in a huff.

Another time she made me a skirt and said to Klares "I have made a deep hem because Karin Ann is going to grow taller and generous seams because Kerstin is going to grow fatter!"

Luckily we were usually able to laugh at her comments; her final one to me was regarding the VW camper van Nick and I bought to drive to Australia.

GRANNY

KLARES & BERTIE

VISITING GRANNY

"My son had one like that but not such a gaudy affair!"

The van was beige, likewise its interior fit out. It was hard to work out what was gaudy about it but I didn't ask.

Sadly, I never saw any sign of her adventurous spirit nor did she tell me about her early life and numerous siblings. Two of her sisters lived in London; aunt Elsa died in a concentration camp during World War 2. What had she spoken to Nietzsche about and what was the journey down the River Ankobra like, in a boat rowed by handsome smiling African youths? I wish I had asked!

Post script

On our last visit, before we left for Australia, Granny started talking about Antwerp and a sea crossing she had made during the war. Gun fire, total mayhem, no one told them what to do, the sky was red. She had been caught up in some kind of bombardment and was only just able to escape.

She was starting to suffer from dementia and though the story sounded intriguing we didn't go into any details with her. After all, when would this have happened? As far as I knew, she spent the whole of the Second World War in London.

Nicholas and I have finally come up with the following theory. Granny had mentioned Antwerp where a major battle had taken place when Germany invaded Belgium at the start of World War One.

Britain declared war with Germany when Germany invaded Belgium, early in August 1914. Before that date, the situation was already volatile. Maybe Granny and Grandfather had already decided to send the two older boys to school in neutral Switzerland to keep them out of harms way. Granny might have been in Berlin making the arrangements but then things happened more quickly than she had anticipated. She hurriedly packed the two boys off with their aunt, obviously a last minute arrangement as they had to leave in a special train with all the blinds drawn down as it made its way through Germany.

Then she had to take herself and the two youngest boys, aged three and one, back to England. She probably wanted to be in England herself so she could still keep in contact with her husband in West Africa. She might not have made it to Antwerp for the channel crossing before the beginning of August, by which time Germany started to invade neutral Belgium. The Battle of Antwerp took place on August 3rd and Granny's tale of gunfire, turmoil and general mayhem could very well have been her desperate escape from the beginning of what was known in those days as the Great War.

As people get older and start suffering from dementia, memories from the past become more vivid than recent happenings. She had never spoken about this before and maybe this was a memory she had wanted to suppress but was now resurfacing.

By Christmas 1915 she was in Seccondee with her husband and two youngest children. My grandfather wrote a letter to his two sons in Switzerland and told them how the family was going to celebrate. Later, on the ship back to England, my grandfather appears to have contracted some illness and he died in port on one of the Canary Islands.

BERTIE WITH GRANDFATHER'S PHOTO

BERTIE WITH PRINCE POLSKI